Dear Barb & Neil
from: Loraine & Trev
x x x

DISCOVERING
BIRDS

D0974289

Also by Tony Soper

The bird table book

The Shell book of beachcombing

Wildlife begins at home

Everyday birds

Beside the sea (with Hilary Soper)

Birdwatch

Penguins (with John Sparks)

Owls: their natural and unnatural history (with John Sparks)

DISCOVERING BIRDS

A practical guide to birdcraft

Tony Soper

Illustrated by Kevin Baker

BBC PUBLICATIONS

For Jack

This book accompanies the BBC Continuing Education Television series
Discovering Birds, first shown on BBC2 in Spring 1983

Series produced by Ron Bloomfield and presented by Tony Soper

Published to accompany a series of programmes
prepared in consultation with the
BBC Continuing Education Advisory Council

This book is set on 10 on 13 point Souvenir Light (Linotron)
Printed in Great Britain by Thomson Litho Ltd, East Kilbride, Scotland
Cover printed by Belmont Press Ltd, Harlestone, Northampton
Bound by Thomson Litho Ltd, East Kilbride, Scotland

© The Author 1983
First published 1983. Reprinted 1983 (three times), 1986
Published by BBC Publications, a division of BBC Enterprises Limited,
35 Marylebone High Street, London W1M 4AA

ISBN 0 563 16555 3

Contents

Acknowledgments

Many people have helped with the compilation of material for this book, among them Chris Mead and David Glue of the British Trust for Ornithology; Stan Davies, Mike Everett and Roger Lovegrove of the Royal Society for the Protection of Birds; Brian Hawkes, Jim Flegg, Robin Prytherch; the staff of the Dartmouth branch of Devon County Library. The Game Conservancy kindly allowed use of material from their booklet entitled 'Wildfowl Management on Inland Waterways'; John Downer and Mike Beynon allowed use of material from the BBC Television children's programme *Wildtrack*; Dr M. J. Isaac of the Swansea Museum helped unravel the history of pigeon houses; Pamela Hanks, of the publishers David & Charles, kindly allowed me to use material from my own *Bird Table Book* and *Everyday Birds*. Gordon Watson, Keeper of Social History at the City of Wakefield Museum, shed light on the splendid work of Charles Waterton; and lastly I must thank my friends and colleagues – Dan Freeman, Tina Clark and Ron Bloomfield – who so nobly shouldered the task of seeing the accompanying film series through both the painful and pleasurable stages of production.

Tony Soper

Dartmouth
July 1982

List of illustrations

9

Introduction

Birds come in most shapes and sizes. With the benefit of millions of years of research and development, they have learnt to take advantage of every food source offered by both the plant kingdom and their fellow animals. Some have specialised in living close to man, thus becoming our mess-mates and sharing the crumbs from our table. Many more enjoy the fruits of our labour indirectly, finding food and shelter in landscapes which are largely created to our specifications, while others suffer as a result of those same drastic changes to the environment. The object of this book is to explore some of the ways in which we may exert our influence to improve the quality of bird life and to enjoy a closer relationship with those birds which prove amenable to manipulation.

Enticing garden birds to the bird table for food and to nestboxes for breeding is highly entertaining for us and, from the birds' point of view, a profitable arrangement. The procedure is by no means confined to the traditional milieu of suburban gardens; wherever there are birds to be found there are ways of improving facilities in such a way that both their lives and our own are enriched.

Birds and birdwatching embrace an extraordinary range of potential interests. The scientific study of bird populations and life-styles provides endless material for professional ornithologists, working in a field which covers the gamut from pure academic research to pest control in the everyday world of agriculture. The amateur birdwatcher's interests may range from disciplined census work through a fairly casual enjoyment of a weekend hobby to the highly-skilled pursuit of rarities by the dedicated and single-minded band of 'twitchers', whose goal is to tick off a longer life-list than the next man in a sporting chase. And there are those of us who simply enjoy the blue tits on the half-coconut, or who write poetry, prose or music about birds. Their fascination is endless. Much of their charm lies in the way their life-styles run on similar paths to our own, though they enjoy the inestimable advantage of flight capability, the facility which we so greatly envy. Unlike the mammals which are our much closer relatives, birds mostly live in our daylight world of sights and sounds, they share a great deal with us, including our food, and this makes it easier to identify with them, albeit at the same time inviting endless problems of the sort which arise when we try to treat them as people.

Birdwatching is a modified form of hunting. Primitive hunters sought only to fill their bellies, but, if we are to enjoy success in our terms we must use their techniques in our aim of getting close to the quarry, both in the literal sense and in that of getting to know them better. To this day the hunter can teach any aspiring birdman a great deal. Fieldcraft involves a great deal more than wearing a battledress jacket. The hunter knows his prey as well as he is able, he moves quietly and with due regard to the wind and the light, above all he knows time and place. Present-day wildlife photographers face all the problems of the hunter, and it is axiomatic that the best ones are those to whom a knowledge of natural history comes first, before knowledge of film stocks and photo apparatus.

The tools of the trade are important. First and foremost are those which are standard issue to all, or at least most of us. Keen eyesight and hearing are the naturalist's most precious assets, followed by an ability to use them effectively. Observation by sight and sound is the basis of all fieldwork. Perhaps the observer's notebook and pencil come next for the best memory in the world is no substitute for on-the-spot recording. Most introductions to birdwatching contain useful sections on field recording, but perhaps the most practical, enjoyable and stimulating is that contained in Ian Wallace's excellent book *Discover birds* published by Whizzard Press/André Deutsch in 1979. Wallace takes the reader on a wild romp to most of Britain's best bird places, and his enthusiasm is both constructive and infectious. His book is one of the rare few which combine scholarship with a light-hearted enjoyment of the subject.

Binoculars are well-nigh indispensable, and they are a source of great heart-searching to many would-be birders. The problem is that, like birds, they come in a bewildering variety of guises. To meet all eventualities, you need to own half-a-dozen pairs. However, given that you are to start by buying one pair, you should go for glasses that are reasonably light in weight and which give a bright picture over a medium field of view. With a magnification of eight, nine or ten times and objective lenses between thirty and fifty millimetres in diameter. Thus your chosen binoculars might be described as 8 × 30 or 9 × 40, both highly suitable everyday combinations. Lower or higher magnifications should go hand in hand with higher light-gathering power, eg 7 × 50 or 10 × 50, the first being ideal for marine use, when you must reduce the problems of unwanted rock and roll, and the second about as powerful as most people can hold without getting a wobbly picture. But see what the people in your local bird club use – you'll learn a lot simply by borrowing their glasses on your first outing or two.

Avoid glasses with magnifications greater than 10 as the plague, until you are experienced enough to use them to advantage. Avoid zoom binoculars which will be heavy and avoid anything which presents you with a blurred image anywhere in the picture or which exhibits colour halo effects. Get the opinions of other birdwatchers and get hold of a field guide pamphlet called *Binoculars and telescopes* published by the British Trust for Ornithology, Beech Grove, Tring, Herts.

Once you have chosen the binocular power which suits you, the best advice is to buy the most expensive you can afford. But during the trial stage it's probably best to enjoy the relatively cheap 'Avocet' glasses marketed by the RSPB. Write to the Sales Dept, RSPB, The Lodge, Sandy, Bedfordshire for a copy of the Sales Catalogue and for membership details. Membership of the Society not only gives your soul the warm glow of satisfaction induced by the knowledge that you are making a highly practical contribution to the well-being of British birds, but brings you a number of benefits, not least of which is the excellent quarterly magazine *Birds*. Local centres, run by the RSPB, provide opportunities to join field excursions, to hear top-class speakers and to see the best of the bird films. It goes without saying that you should also join your local bird club, in order to get the benefit of meeting people who have a strong interest in the bird patch which you share. Local knowledge is vital and is freely shared by genuine birders.

Whether your interest is in far-flung ornithological expeditions or in studying the action nowhere more demanding than your back garden through the kitchen window with a mug of coffee in your hand, you need to be able to make a positive identification of the birds you see or hear. There are several field guides to identification – hunter's manuals – and you must choose the one which suits you best. There are three which are the most widely used. Peterson, Mountford and Hollom's *Field guide to the birds of Britain and Europe* was first published, by Collins, in 1954 and it has enjoyed high approval by birdwatchers. The current edition is completely revised and up to date. It has stood the test of time, and can only really be faulted on its tiresome pagination and layout, which are not designed to make for quick reference. Another Collins field guide, *The birds of Britain and Europe, with North Africa and the Middle East*, by Hermann Heinzel, Fitter and Parslow, published in 1972, is perhaps not to be recommended as a first purchase since it covers a wider geographical area than a beginner birdwatcher ought decently to be interested in. *The Hamlyn guide to the birds of Britain and Europe* by Bertel Bruun, published in 1978, has the great advantage of a conventional layout which marries text, maps and drawings so that they appear on the same page for each bird. Examine all these three before you choose. Incidentally, membership of the RSPB should bring you a chance to get an admirable booklet *What's that bird?*, with pictures by Peter Hayman and a text by Michael Everett which gives a succinct account of 'the most likely birds' and groups them in a useful habitat sequence.

As for general introductions to bird biology and behaviour, there are excellent books by David Saunders (*RSPB guide to British birds* published by Hamlyn, 1975), by Peter Conder (*RSPB guide to birdwatching*, Hamlyn, 1978), by James Fisher and Jim Flegg (*Watching birds*, T. & A. D. Poyser, 1974), and there is even my own offering (*Birdwatch*, Webb & Bower, 1982).

You will also need a more encyclopaedic volume of background information species by species, and this is well catered for by P. A. D. Hollom (*The popular handbook of British birds*, Witherby, n.e. 1968). In due course you will inevitably want copies of the seven-volume *The handbook of the birds of Europe, the Middle East and North Africa*: OUP (*The birds of the Western Palearctic, 1977–81*), mercifully known to birders by the shortened form BWP. So far three volumes have been published of what will inevitably be the standard work of ornithological reference for many years. You will want to keep up to date with the birdwatchers' monthly magazine *British Birds*, a lively and authoritative journal. Write to Mrs Erika Sharrock, Fountains, Park Lane, Blunham, Bedford MK44 3NJ for a free sample copy. And when your birdwatching develops into an unquenchable craving for more knowledge and you initiate your own research you must share your results with the rest of us by submitting them to BB for publication. But I warn you, it is about as easy to get a 'note' into BB as it is to get a letter accepted for *The Times* correspondence page.

Books are notoriously useless at imparting information about the sounds made by birds. Yet their calls and songs are often a vital clue to their identification, to say nothing of their state of mind. Probably the best way to learn the birdsong is by way of a knowlegeable companion. But a good gramophone record or tape will help. Jeffery Boswall has edited a splendid set of vocalisations recorded by Sture Palmer in *A field guide to the birdsongs of Britain and Europe*, which is available (from the RSPB, for instance) in both disc and cassette form. John Kirby's *Wild Track* cassettes are also available from the RSPB.

So, equipped with the tools of the trade and an understanding of the basic principles of bird biology, we may set out to unravel the mysteries of bird management.

Bird topography

Putting a name to a bird is arguably the first requirement in getting to know something about it. And a knowledge of bird topography is an important foundation in the building up of identification expertise. Yet unfortunately the charts published in bird identification manuals offer such varied systems that they may confuse more than they help. The editors of *British Birds* magazine have produced these comprehensive and authoritative 'British Standard' charts in the hope that everyone will use the same language. The drawings are by Peter Grant.

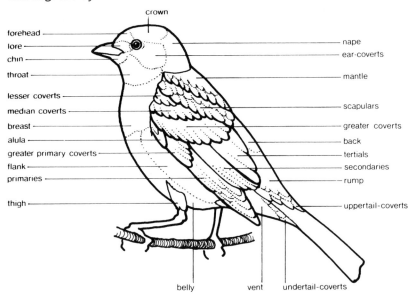

Right: The 'tarsus' is actually the tarsometatarsus; the 'knee' is actually the intertarsal joint; the 'ankle' is actually the tarsometatarsophalangeal joint. We have, however, preferred the anatomically inaccurate but very much simpler and more easily understood terms.

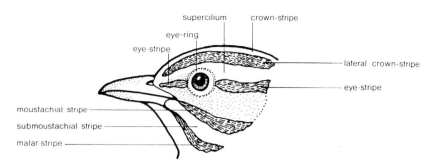

supercilium
crown-stripe
eye-ring
eye-stripe
lateral crown-stripe
eye-stripe
moustachial stripe
submoustachial stripe
malar stripe

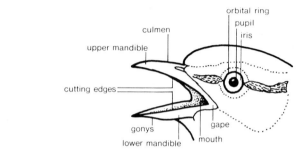

orbital ring
pupil
iris
culmen
upper mandible
cutting edges
gonys
gape
lower mandible
mouth

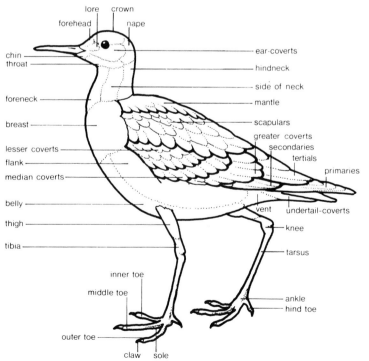

lore
crown
forehead
nape
chin
ear-coverts
throat
hindneck
side of neck
foreneck
mantle
breast
scapulars
greater coverts
secondaries
lesser coverts
tertials
flank
primaries
median coverts
belly
vent
undertail-coverts
thigh
knee
tibia
tarsus
inner toe
middle toe
ankle
hind toe
outer toe
claw
sole

17

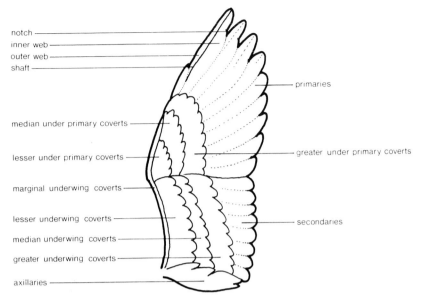

notch
inner web
outer web
shaft

primaries

median under primary coverts

lesser under primary coverts

greater under primary coverts

marginal underwing coverts

lesser underwing coverts

secondaries

median underwing coverts

greater underwing coverts

axillaries

Chart of underwing.

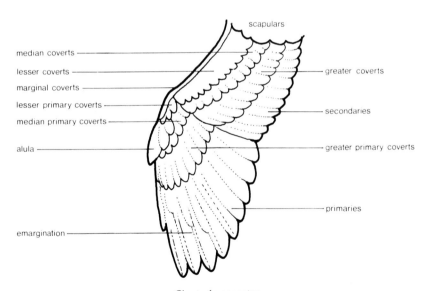

scapulars

median coverts

lesser coverts

marginal coverts

greater coverts

lesser primary coverts

median primary coverts

secondaries

alula

greater primary coverts

primaries

emargination

Chart of upperwing.

Standard bird topography charts reproduced by kind permission
of Peter Grant and the editors of *British Birds* magazine.

ONE
Bird gardening

Historical background

On the grand scale, bird management involves the farming of large acreages in order to provide favourable conditions for resident or visiting species, thus increasing their numbers. The pioneers of this sort of activity worked in America, where suitable lakes and lakeside vegetation are still strictly controlled for the benefit of migratory wildfowl. In Britain, the Royal Society for the Protection of Birds (RSPB) manages a network of bird reserves which, at the same time, serves the purposes of other wildlife. The productive and healthy farming of any habitat will support the liveliest population of birds, so what's good for worms is good for birds, too, in the long run.

It has been said that Saint Cuthbert, living the simple life at his hermitage on Inner Farne, off the Northumberland coast, in the seventh century AD ran the first bird reserve in Britain. His was an all-embracing love, encompassing otters and seals as well as eiders and gannets, to say nothing of his fellow men. He enjoyed all his birds, but had a special affection for the eiders, affording them total protection from the hunters.

Inevitably, the earliest records of active bird management derive from the economic value of the subject. Some centuries ago pigeons were encouraged to breed in convenient coastal caves, for example at Wemyss in Fife (although the practice originated much earlier in the Middle East), in order to take advantage of the resulting fat squabs. And while wildfowl had been hunted and herded in northern countries (during their flightless period of moult), the first account of managed breeding herds in Britain comes from Abbotsbury in Dorset. Here the monks of the Benedictine Monastery encouraged the nesting mute swans, taking a proportion of the fat cygnets for the table. The first written records of this activity were in 1393. The swans did well on the rich feeding in the coastal lagoons of the Fleet, inside Chesil Bank. In 1543, Henry VIII granted the right to keep the herd to the Fox

Strangways family, who have protected the swans through the years to the present day. The swanherd watches over a flock which numbers some 400 to 500 birds at breeding time, but rises to nearer 1000 in winter.

It was Squire Charles Waterton, of Walton Hall near Wakefield in Yorkshire, who deliberately set out to create a bird park of his property and thus probably became the proprietor of the first nature reserve in Britain to be established for pleasure and enjoyment. In 1817, he began a ten-year plan which systematically developed his 260 acres into a sanctuary designed to improve the prospects for birds. He banned shooting altogether, threatening to strangle his gamekeeper if he shot any barn owls, and forbade boating on his lake during the waterfowl breeding season. He also built a high wall round the entire property to exclude casual disturbance, and dogs. Foxes were trapped and deported, and even badgers were shown the door, in rather drastic moves to reduce the hazards to birds. Curiously, though, he encouraged weasels, inveterate small-bird killers, but this was because he had an obsession with ridding the estate of the abundant brown rats, the 'Hanoverian' rats which he hated.

Walton Hall, from the lake.
Probably the first nature reserve in Britain.

Charles Waterton, the squire of Walton Hall, at the age of 42.

Waterton's enclosed reserve, and his management of it, was highly successful. In a letter to his friend George Ord, dated 1849, he wrote: '... my
carrion crows, herons, hawks and magpies have done very well this year
and I have a fine brood of kingfishers. They may thank their stars that they
have my park wall to protect them. But for it their race would be extinct in
this depraved and demoralized part of Yorkshire.'

He experimented with various kinds of nestbox designed to encourage
owls (and starlings!) to breed. He ensured, too, the luxurious growth of ivy,

correctly deciding that it was a wholly beneficial plant which would provide food and shelter for the birds without damaging his trees. One way or another Squire Waterton was far in advance of his contemporaries in understanding the general principles of wildlife management on an ecological basis, in spite of his aberrations. He successfully sued the owners of a nearby soap works when he considered their effluent was polluting his lake, but the law, reflecting the spirit of an age when industry was of key importance, awarded him derisory damages. Yet interestingly, Waterton's relations with fellow workers in his field were inclined to be fairly hot-tempered. He cordially despised the museum workers, calling them 'closet naturalists' (this was at a time when taxonomy, the science of classification, was the only fit pursuit for a professional), and positively gloried in field-work as well as his amateur status. When he shot birds for his collection (he was an enthusiastic taxidermist) he chose only males, because he preferred the bright colours! However, in an age when estates were kept up primarily for the production of game, and keepers were almost without exception wedded to the concept of vermin destruction with little understanding of the relationship between species, Waterton's ideas were regarded as highly eccentric, an epithet which he firmly rejected but invited time and time again by indulging in a series of bizarre exploits. One of his many party tricks in later life was to scratch the back of his head with the big toe of his right foot. He must bear his share of responsibility for the long-standing belief that naturalists are not entirely stable creatures.

By the end of his time Waterton had recorded 122 species of birds in his park, including osprey, hobby, hooded crow and crossbill. Sadly, after his death the estate was bought by a man who 'improved' it back to conventional tidiness and ruined Waterton's life's work.

Aims of the bird gardener

Large scale bird management tends to be connected with agriculture, or sport (in the field of game conservation). But there is plenty of potential for influencing the lives of birds so that their lot is improved and our enjoyment of their company increased. And, for this process, the term 'bird gardening' is a convenient one, whether the area in question is around a factory, a school playing-field, or the garden of a house. Man's works inevitably attract their quota of wildlife, just as inevitably as they deprive some species of their living space – they not only diminish, but provide opportunities. The bird gardener seeks to enhance these possibilities. After all, the birds will come whether we like it or not, so we might as well enjoy them. And by providing new possibilities we may reverse the trend towards impoverishment in terms of species diversity.

Quite apart from their practical usefulness in terms of pest control and as agents of seed dispersal, birds are important to us as a food source. But not only are they useful, they are beautiful as well. Their colour and movement, their calls and songs add whole new dimensions to existence. So the diligent bird gardener sets out to please them and to organise a welcome. Put simply, this means providing food, water and shelter.

Food is the prime requirement of any animal. As fuel, it provides energy, promotes health, allows for defence capability and the capacity for repro-duction. Water is equally important, not just for drinking but as a necessary requirement in the maintenance of plumage. Shelter provides protection from enemies and the elements, and serves as a nursery. A long-established, mature garden with a diversity of shrubs and flowering plants, with a mix of young, prime and decaying trees, some clad in ivy, an orchard with lichen-encrusted apple trees and surrounded by thick impenetrable hedges, allied to a house with plenty of corners and ledges, to say nothing of cracks and crevices, is already a most productive bird haven. The highest bird density in Britain is found in suburban gardens and estates, where the habitat resembles an endless woodland edge, one which lacks the less 'birdy' forest interior. But it has to be recognised that this habitat doesn't suit all species, so special attention needs to be given to those which have been dispossessed by house building. This is why the bird gardener also supports the intensive work done by organisations like the RSPB.

Faced with the prospect of a newly built house, surrounded by a morass of subsoil, you must obviously survey the situation carefully before rushing into a planting programme. First of all, make sure that your precious topsoil is carefully replaced. Ensure, also, that any existing boundary walls or hedges, and other features such as trees, ponds or wells, are carefully preserved, so that you are able to write them into your plan. Determine the soil type, consider the orientation of the ground, and cast a long look at the biological opportunities that abut onto your property. While your neigh-bours may jealously guard their territorial rights, wilder animals will use the highways which suit their purposes without any consideration for property law. The object is to reinforce the positive advantages of your own patch, to introduce complementary possibilities, and to exert what influence you can on the neighbouring land. If there is a public park nearby, for instance, it may be worth encouraging the authorities to improve their tree-planting

plans by concentrating on native trees, thus discouraging those dark and dismal laurel/rhododendron plantations.

In the garden, the object should be to plant for maximum nut, berry, seed and insect production, to provide a measure of cover, and to provide water. In a newly planted garden, which will inevitably lack abundant bird food, a bird table will be most important, but the long-term plan should be to provide as varied and plentiful a mix of natural food as possible. Make the place an adventure course for enterprising bird explorers. A varied terrain of lawns, rockeries, walls, miniature hills, valleys, streams and ponds. If the visiting birds find a rich cornucopia, they are more likely to move in and settle.

Above: song thrush and rowan berries.
Left: A mature bird garden offers food and shelter.

The process starts with an abundance of greenery, providing food for insects which in turn support blue-tits, which in their turn support sparrowhawks. The very nature of gardening itself, the process of turning soil and planting new life, encourages a particular group of birds – those which are best able to adapt to our activities. Robins, thrushes, sparrows,

Robins take advantage of any mammal which
conveniently exposes worm-rich soil for them.

starlings and dunnocks are all predisposed to live alongside us and will soon take advantage of new housing estates. On the other hand, many of our summer visitors, such as warblers, need to be encouraged, by providing a wealth of foliage and flowers which support quantities of insects.

A variety of 'weeds'

Seriously consider the possibility of keeping a wilderness area in part of your garden, a wild jungle of weeds and shrubs which can be visited by hunting bands of itinerant finches. A clump of nettles will be a hothouse breeding-ground for insects and spiders, and the leaves will serve as egg-laying sites for butterflies. If possible, the wilderness area should have a dark and secret roosting-place where birds may rest and recuperate, but the most important factor is a flourishing variety of seed-producing 'weeds'.

Nettles are good value – and beautiful, too. Other suitable plants are thistles, knapweed, teazel, ragwort, groundsel, chickweed, dandelion and dock. Although these sound like a veritable catalogue of disaster, the advantage of these native plants is that they offer first-class feeding opportunities to our birds which are well equipped to exploit them. Goldfinches use their long probing bills to extract the seeds from prickly thistle and teazel

One man's weed is another man's dinner.
Chiffchaffs hunt insects in a nettle-patch...

... while goldfinches extract seeds from thistle heads.

heads. It is true that wild thistles have an unfortunate tendency to run riot, but the ornamental varieties, which are most restrained territorially, still produce plenty of seeds. Cow parsley, that vigorous and glorious hedgerow edge plant, should be a welcome member of the wilderness community and greenfinches much enjoy its seeds. And the same is true of fat hen, a plant cordially disliked by 'real' gardeners but equally cordially enjoyed by finches when they go for the seeds in late summer.

Bramble should find a place somewhere. Apart from providing good roosting and nesting potential, its flowers support insects, comma caterpillars feed on its leaves and, in due course, thrushes and blackbirds take the berries, voiding the pips which in their turn are found by passing finches.

Trees and shrubs

Obviously, your ability to nurture trees will depend on the size of your plot, and it is true that plenty of low, dense cover is far more important in a small garden. But if you can possibly find room for it, grow one tall tree – for instance a poplar – which will serve as a song post for a thrush. But even if denied a natural song perch, your thrush or blackbird will happily accept the second-best option of a chimney pot or television aerial. And if you are lucky enough to have an old decaying tree on your patch, then cherish it for any number of reasons which will become apparent. Felling should only be regarded as a last resort, in cases of potential danger. Enjoy the well-grown trees you have, plant new ones for your grandchildren.

Where you have space to plant new trees, choose native species by preference rather than the exotics which nurserymen will be only too glad to recommend. The foliage, fruits and seeds of native trees will be more efficiently harvested by our birds, which are programmed by long experience to utilise them to best advantage. Be careful to consider their eventual size when you are planting specimens which seem puny at the time. So allow space, but allow for thinning.

Our native trees are better able to withstand our moist and wayward weather, and harmonise well with the other plants and animals in their community. Mature oaks and limes support a flourishing community of their own, but of course they do take time to grow. 'Two hundred years a-growing, two hundred a-thinking and two hundred a-dying' just about sums up an oak's life, but for all that people think of it in terms of slow growth, it can reach a goodly girth and height well within one man's lifetime. In forest conditions an oak may reach up 130 ft (40 m), but a lime may exceed that

Thrushes prefer to sing from a high vantage point, the uppermost twig
of a poplar, for instance, or the television aerial on a chimney.

by yet another 30 ft (9 m). The lime, however, is very amenable to pruning,
and as one of the few forest trees to be pollinated by insects, it hums with
activity in summer. One particular aphid chooses limes on which to enjoy
sap and exude its sticky honey-dew, attracting queues of bees and other
insects. So naturally it is a favourite with birds, which also enjoy its autumn
fruits.

If you are looking for trees which will grow fast and provide a quick return
for garden birds, choose ash, elm, birch, willow and native cherry. Ash
grows rapidly in any soil, and its seeds – keys – are an important food source
for bullfinches and others. Birch, too, will grow fast in most soils, but it is
somewhat disease-prone, an advantage perhaps for the bird gardener who
lives in the hope of providing woodpeckers with an easily drilled home. Its
seeds are eagerly taken by redpolls, siskins and tits. For smaller gardens
there is a dwarf version, *Betula pendula youngii*, a weeping birch.

The purple berries of elder are enjoyed by dozens of species of birds, so it
clearly merits a place in any birdman's garden. The native form is preferable
to cultivars, it grows fast, almost anywhere, and it is hardy, taking plenty of
punishment. Since its leaves appear early in the season it provides valuable
nesting cover for our native songbirds, which breed earlier than the migrant
visitors.

Ideally, trees in a garden should exhibit a mixed age structure, with young trees allowing plenty of light to reach the ground plants and prime trees providing an abundance of food and shelter. In the long run, decaying trees are the most valuable of all, allowing living space and providing sustenance to the greatest variety and number of insects and plants which live off their bounty. If you find the spectacle of a slowly dying tree a trifle uncomfortable, then clothe it with ivy to make it look more interesting!

Fruit trees in an orchard supply large quantities of bird food, both in terms of insects and, more controversially, the fruit itself. But it may be possible to leave some of the fruit on a few of the trees, so that it will decay gently into the kind of soft flesh for which thrushes are so grateful in the winter. In summer, blue tits will hunt over apple trees and take quantities of the codling moth caterpillars which cause so much damage. Both apples and pears suit birds very well, as do most other fruits. Wild cherry is a satisfactory bird tree, but avoid the sterile double-flowered cultivated varieties. Blackbirds and starlings, too, will be pleased to help you harvest redcurrant and flowering currants. Of course, it is easy to object to the way birds take their tithe of fruit and table vegetables, but the other side of the coin is a valid one; starlings, for instance, eat large numbers of leatherjackets.

In the breeding season, starlings take quantities
of worms, leatherjackets, woodlice, slugs and snails.

Spindle is a useful shrub, growing as much as 15 ft (4.6 m) high. Bushy and ornamental, it prefers chalky or lime-rich soil. In autumn it sports attractive colours, after producing a rich crop of pink and orange fruit. However, this fruit is poisonous to humans and should not be planted if you have young children. But rowan (mountain ash) is a first-class bird tree: it needs plenty of light but is not fussy, although it prefers a light soil. Fruiting in August, its brilliant coral-red fruits are a magnet for mistle thrushes, blackbirds, song thrushes and starlings, which will strip the tree long before winter. A useful bonus with rowan is that it will provide protection for your property against the evil designs of any passing witch. And if the extensive rowan berry crops of Scandinavia fail, then in winter eastern Britain sometimes enjoys an invasion of the spectacular waxwings, birds which depend upon the berries and hunt rather desperately through our hedgerows in search of substitutes.

Hedges are very important to birds, providing endless opportunities – for both food and shelter. So it is worth spending some time and effort on growing satisfactory ones. If possible, the ideal is to mix the plants so that they provide a range of food choices which peak at different times of the year. Hawthorn, for example, makes a good basic choice. As a free-growing

A hawthorn hedge provides fruit in autumn and secret
nesting places in spring. Bullfinch and family.

31

tree it will grow quite tall, but it bows gracefully to life as a disciplined hedge – cut to shape, layered and trimmed it provides dense cover. It grows quickly, almost anywhere, and its spiny branches soon form an excellent boy-proof barrier. It presents lovely colour in spring, while its secret interior houses songbirds' nests. From August it provides a generous crop of scarlet haws, luscious berries which are taken by thrushes and blackbirds, as well as winter visitors like fieldfares and redwings, to say nothing of waxwings. Be careful not to confuse it with blackthorn, whose sloes are not much liked by birds.

Holly is another first-class hedge plant, although it is reluctant to fruit when it is hard clipped, and it prefers well-drained soil. It may be a slow grower, so make a point of buying vigorous (and expensive) stock from the nurserymen. If you are free-growing it for berries, make sure you plant females, but there must be one pollinating male nearby to be sure of effective fertilisation. The cultivated forms are most reliable. 'Golden King' (a female) grows to 10 ft (3 m) and crops well; 'Madame Briot' to 18 ft (5.5 m), producing golden berries. As a hedge plant, holly mixes well, providing a good evergreen cat-proof hedge with an impenetrable roosting and nesting fastness. Birds are not enthusiastic about the berries, except in hard weather, but the holly hedge pays its way by virtue of its secure winter roosting potential.

Hazel is a useful addition to the hedgerow, on the grounds of diversity in that it provides a welcome nut harvest in August and September. It flourishes best on rich, chalky soils which are not too wet. Find a sunny space or two for some crab-apple trees in the hedge, as they are an invaluable source of winter food for thrushes in hard weather. Fieldfares and redwings will enjoy the flesh, leaving the pips for finches. The fruit resembles outsize yellow cherries and is reluctant to fall, even after the leaves have been shed, thus providing good food very late in the winter. There are various ornamental versions but it is probably best to stick to the native wild crab apple *Malus pumila*, though an ornamental variety 'Golden Hornet' has been recommended for its abundant crop of small yellow fruits, much appreciated by thrushes. Tits work hard to get at the pips, and chaffinches take the pips after the fruits have been hacked open by thrushes. The variety 'Veitches scarlet' produces large, scarlet fruits.

Yew is another useful hedgerow plant. It will suffer endless clipping and live a long and fruitful life as a 6 ft (1.8 m) bush. (Though if you let it, it will live a thousand years and grow to 90 ft (27.5 m).) The foliage and bark, as well as the seeds, are poisonous to domestic stock so it is not suitable for

Leave some apple windfalls to provide food
for winter visitors like fieldfares.

farm hedges. However, it serves well in a bird garden. The evergreen hedge provides useful nest-sites and the fleshy red berries of the female tree provide good feeding for thrushes and starlings which eat the pulp and pass on the poisonous seed without harm. Remember, incidentally, to introduce males into the hedge, though in some instances both male and female flowers appear on the same tree. Of course, a close-clipped hedge plant will not fruit as generously as a free-growing tree, but a well-varied boundary of evergreen and deciduous fruit, together with nut-bearing plants is a decided advantage from the birds' point of view. Do your hedging and ditching, tree lopping and any necesary felling early in the year, certainly by the end of March, and then the birds will not be disturbed at nesting time.

Climbing plants

Trees, whether they are free-standing or part of a hedge system, may be much improved by teaming them with climbing plants. And if considerations of space, or respect for your neighbour's view, mean that you cannot have trees at all, then at least erect some trellis or fencing to provide something for a climber to conquer.

Honeysuckle is a liana which will entwine and climb, providing a colourful display of early flowers and heady fragrance, but in the process will allow for some secret nest-places. Its nectar is attractive to privet hawk-moths which reach it with long probosci; blackbirds, tits and blackcaps are not enthusiastic but will take the berries. *Lonicera fragrantissima* grows bushy and is suitable as a sunny hedgerow plant; *L. periclymenum*, the native woodbine, is the entwiner and prefers some shade.

The much-maligned and ill-treated ivy should be treated with respect and cherished in any birdman's garden. Castigated by the ignorant as a strangler of trees, it in fact does no harm except in the very rare cases when it completely covers the crown and cuts off light to the foliage. It is also frequently said that ivy sucks the goodness out of any tree which it climbs. This is untrue: ivy takes no nourishment, neither does it restrict the rate of growth of its 'host'. The fact is that ivy is a top-class birdman's plant. Thriving even in poor soil, it will carpet the ground till it finds an opportunity to climb. The dense, leathery leaves do not have the fragile beauty of any number of exotic imports, nevertheless they are a robust part of the British garden and woodland scene. Climbing by virtue of the deceptively root-like hairs on its stem, ivy flowers when it reaches light. Flowering late, in September and

Ivy is one of the bird gardener's best friends.

October, it offers rich nectar at a time when this scarce commodity is particularly appreciated by butterflies, bees and other insects. Similarly, ivy fruits exceptionally late, in March and April, when its berries supply desperately needed late winter food for wood pigeons and thrushes, to say nothing of a number of small mammals. Aside from this virtue, which should guarantee ivy a welcome in every garden, its convolutions and evergreen secret places provide a rich source of nest sites and roosting places. Through the year, its hairy stems and nourishing leaves support quantities of insects, which in turn provide food for hunting wrens and tits. The 'Irish ivy' is a good cover for north-facing walls. A rampant grower, it is dense and grows out from the wall in bush shapes, providing not only exceptionally good roosting places but free thermal insulation for the house as well.

Evergreens

Apart from food and, for some species, water as well, one of the important bird functions of greenery in a garden is to provide roosting shelter at night, especially in winter. So, as well as ivy, it is worth making sure that you have a fair proportion of evergreens in your garden, for instance in the boundary hedge. Even laurel and rhododendron are useful in this respect. Town councils like them because they shade the ground and inhibit the growth of weeds, but they nurture few insects and offer little food value. Both common and white spruce make useful roost trees and offer good nest-sites as well. If you are lucky enough to have a *Wellingtonia* (and if you plant one

Treecreeper roosting in *Wellingtonia*

remember it grows to be the biggest tree in the world – in its native California it is known modestly as the 'Big Tree'), cherish it as the preferred roost tree for tree creepers. They excavate an egg-shaped burrow in the spongy fibrous bark, then repair to it for the night, tucking themselves into the hollow in a vertical posture, bill resting on the bark and tail down, feathers fluffed out boldly – a most astonishing sight. *Wellingtonia* was introduced to Britain in 1853 (the year after the Duke of Wellington died). Before this time tree creepers made hollows in rotting trees, or utilised natural cavities or crevices behind loose bark, as of course large numbers of them still do. But it is relatively easy to discover them on *Wellingtonia*, sometimes as many as a dozen or so, low down on the same tree.

Deciduous and evergreen shrubs and climbers

Various forms of *Cotoneaster* are useful, as ground-huggers, bushes and climbers, because they are insect-rich as well as providing a cornucopia of berries. *C. interimma* fruits conveniently late, between the hawthorn and ivy harvests. Thrushes, finches and tits enjoy its rich red berries and it grows almost anywhere. Useful cultivated forms include:

> *C. simonsii*. Effective hedge plant, produces good bird berries.
> *C. horizontalis*. Deciduous. Fan-shaped cover for wall. Height up to 10 ft (3 m) if against wall. Red berries last well into winter.
> *C. bullata*. 'Cornubia'. Height and spread 6 ft to 15 ft (1.8 m to 4.6 m). Deciduous. Clusters of red berries on arching branches.
> *C. conspicua*. Sometimes known as *C. wardii*. Grows 4 ft to 6 ft (1.2 m to 1.8 m) Grey foliage and orange berries.
> *C. dammeri* and *C. prostrata*. Small, ground-hugging, ever spreading trailers. Good ground cover, encouraging bugs.
> *C. buxifolia*. Evergreen wall climber, to 5 ft (1.5 m).
> *C. francheti*. Evergreen wall climber, to 10 ft (3 m).
> *C. lactea*. Evergreen wall climber to 15 ft (4.6 m).
> *C. aldenhamensis*. Slowly grows to small tree.
> *C. watereri*. Slowly grows to small tree.

Like *Cotoneaster*, the common barberry also shows itself in a bewildering variety of forms – full species and hybrids. But all of them offer rich pickings for birds, as well as colourful foliage which provides thick ground cover inhibiting weed growth. *Berberis vulgaris*, the common barberry, is a deciduous plant, branching thickly and growing to 6 ft (1.8 m), providing

may be shredded by greenfinches looking for the seeds. The guelder rose, *Viburnum opulus*, produces clusters of red berries which may be reluctantly taken by birds. It grows to 18 ft (5.5 m), but there is a cultivated version, *V. compactum* which grows to 6 ft (1.8 m). The Japanese snowball, *V. tomentosum plicatum*, is sterile and useless from a bird's point of view. The wild rose, *Rosa rugosa*, produces good fruits and is much to be preferred to the more modern and showy varieties which are selected for colour, shape and scent at the expense of anything which might please either bee or bird. In other words, roses are an abomination to the bird gardener, to be compared with the equally unproductive tulips, dahlias and similar plants which offer a waste land to birds. The general rule is to prefer native species to exotics. Buy British!

Lawns and lawn-watching

An open and well-kept lawn is a priceless asset to the bird-rich garden. It provides a courting arena for pigeons, a battleground for blackbirds, not to mention a great deal of choice food. Artificial and man-made though it may be, the green sward of the lawn, clearly observable and yet a constant

Cock blackbirds use the lawn as a jousting
arena in their territorial chases.

attraction to bug, beast and bird, is a boon to the naturalist-gardener. Curious that this green invitation to laze and relax is the result of such brutal treatment to an inoffensive plant. The constant cutting down of its efforts to reach maturity is hard on the grass, and to add insult to injury we cart off the cuttings to rot elsewhere, depriving the lawn of the very nutrients which aid its survival. Of course, these are replenished to a certain extent by the activity of soil bacteria and by the considerable efforts of worms, but over the years mowing will impoverish the soil if you deny it the cuttings. That is why, if you want to avoid bare patches, you need to import manures to counteract nitrogen deficiency. Again, if you cut too often and too close you will be providing conditions favourable to ground-hugging plants like dandelions, daisies and plantains. So give the grass a chance and keep the weeds in the shade, which doesn't suit them at all. Incidentally, the compost heap provides good pickings in that it is a hothouse of insect-food production and a highly productive wormery. In winter its warmth may keep a small area free of snow and provide a welcome hunting ground.

Lawn-watching offers the easiest way of observing some of the different techniques used by birds for feeding. One of the constant wonders of the natural world is its diversity, the extraordinary range of plants and animals in any given habitat, and the way that they all manage to make a living by

Birds come in all shapes and sizes.
1 Bullfinch, a seed eater.   2 Little owl, nocturnal hunter.
3 Robin, insect eater.   4 Swallow, aerial hunter.
5 Black-headed gull, general purpose feeder.

occupying slightly different niches. Superficially, the 'nature red in tooth and claw' approach may seem justified, but it would be more accurate to see communities of different creatures living in tolerable harmony. Birds come in all shapes and sizes. Some hunt by day, some by night; some are vegetarian, some are meat eaters; some eat anything they can get hold of, including other birds. They may walk after their food, hop for it, fly for it, dive or swim for it. And each is specially equipped for the chosen job. One way or another anything which grows or moves gets eaten. Fruit, nuts, seeds, leaves, bark, living or decaying matter – all is grist to the mill. Very roughly we can divide birds into four categories according to the shape of their beaks: the hard-billed birds like sparrows, or finches which have nutcracker bills; the soft-billed birds, like robins, which deal with insects; the dual-purpose bills which take on all-comers; and the hook-billed predators like sparrowhawks.

On the lawn, the most obvious visitors are the birds searching for worms and soft grubs. The old saying about the early bird getting the worm is an exact observation of fact. Worms are creatures of moisture and mildness, early morning dew suits them, sunrise and sun warmth causes them to return underground. So thrushes and blackbirds comb the lawn at first light, and this is when you may see the bigger blackbird steal worms from the song thrush, thus getting his breakfast the easy way.

Birds have a good sense of hearing, but they hunt almost entirely by the sense of sight, and to some extent touch – at least that is true of those most active by day. When the thrush catches a worm, he does it because he has seen it first. The frequent false observation that birds 'listen' for worms is based on a characteristic human weakness: people make the classic mistake of regarding birds, or any other animal for that matter, as if they, too, were people. The worm-hunting thrush hops a few paces, then stands very still and cocks its head to one side. A pause, and then the stab. So we deduce that the bird had its head cocked to listen for the sound of the worm. But the observer failed to take note of the fact that the bird's *eye* happens to be in the position where the human *ear* is found. When a man cocks his head in that attitude he is listening intently. When a thrush does it, he is watching intently.

There is another procedure which sometimes produces good returns for birds. If a mole is busy at his underground activities, disturbing surface lines as it tunnels, thrushes and blackbirds will keep station on the mole, enjoying the worms which are displaced. This sort of activity, where one species benefits from the activities of another – known as commensalism – is much more common than we realise.

A hen blackbird watches intently in the hope of
catching a worm, while a mole tunnels away underneath.

The bird which is a universal favourite when he swoops onto a lawn is the
green woodpecker, with his striking green plumage and red head. His
curious flight – a few flaps followed by a glide, with wings clasped tight to the
body – and yaffling call, bring him switchbacking into the garden. So remarkable is his appearance that many people find it difficult to believe that
he is a British bird at all, working on the dismal assumption that home-grown
species are bound to be dull and dowdy. But British he is, and a delight to
see, working over the lawn and exploring for ants and ants' nests.

The other woodpeckers, equally striking in their red-and-white livery, are
less attracted to ground level, but the green woodpecker, with his long,
mobile tongue tipped with sticky mucus, searches out larvae from their
hidey-holes in crevices. He may spear out larger bugs, but ants are his
speciality.

Some of the lawn visitors are looking for grass and weed seeds, and of
these perhaps the most attractive is the goldfinch. The sight of a charm of
goldfinches attacking the golden dandelions ought to be enough to convert
any gardener into a dandelion fan. They approach them with zest, leapfrog-
ging onto stems, landing about halfway up towards the head so that they

weigh it down to the ground. Then they get to work. All finches are seed-eaters, with powerful jaw muscles and bills modified for husking. They have two grooves inside the bill which locate the nut or seed, then the tongue rotates it as the mandibles crush. The husk peels off, leaving the kernel to be swallowed. Different finches go for different seeds, a hawfinch for example is tough enough to cope with cherry and plum stones, which take some cracking. Goldfinches, at the weaker end of the finch scale, use their relatively long, narrow bills rather as a pair of tweezers, probing deep into the seedhead.

Swallows will occasionally settle on a lawn to pick up flies if they are abundant, but most of the time they are concerned with airborne flies. Perhaps the most spectacular lawn visitor, but one you're only likely to see if you live on the south coast, is the hoopoe. With its pinkish-brown plumage, barred black on the wings and back, it swoops onto the grass with a lazy flight. On landing it shows a remarkable crest in the shape of a fan, pink with black tips. Then it struts about, probing into the soil with its long, decurved

Hoopoe, with erect crest.

bill. Typically, it prefers parkland, orchard and open-wooded country, but it is found in the vicinity of houses where it feeds on lawns and paths for insect larvae. A very few stay with us to nest, in holes in trees or buildings, and some years there is a considerable influx of them. One of the hoopoe's most endearing traits is its tameness and tolerance of man: even the French are fond of it and refrain from shooting. Its name derives from its voice – a low, but penetrating, sexy hoop-oop-oop. The scientific name *Upupa epops* is both onomatopoeic and charming at the same time.

TWO
Birds and bird tables

The most satisfying way of increasing the bird population in your garden is by growing the right kind of plants and creating as near a wild environment for them as possible. But there is a great deal of pleasure and enjoyment to be derived from providing food in the most direct manner, by setting a dining-table and serving suitable dishes. And almost any food we offer, from kitchen scraps to caviar, will be eaten by a wide variety of birds ranging from tomtits to goshawks.

Birds approve of the provision of bird tables, though
some are more welcome than others. Starlings sweep
the board by force of numbers and personality.

Early enthusiasts

While it is entirely possible to make out a case for feeding birds in order to improve their chances of surviving natural or unnatural disasters, the reason most of us do it is because we enjoy interfering in other creatures' lives and establishing closer relationships with them. Francis of Assisi was probably the first man to be credited with feeding birds from a relatively pure sense of goodwill. After a wild youth, he repented to take a vow of poverty and to devote his life to a form of pilgrimage, helping the poor. The poor, in this context, included the brute creation which doubtless enjoyed the Franciscan's bounty without adopting his principles of poverty, chastity and obedience.

To the best of our knowledge, the first man to set up a bird table unselfishly dedicated to the sustenance of birds was John Freeman Dovaston, an early pioneer of field ornithology. In a letter to the artist Thomas Bewick in 1825, he mentioned his 'ornithotrophe', a feeding device which he had erected outside a window, to which he had enticed twenty-three species to take food on a snowy day. Over a quarter of a century later, the Rev. F. O. Morris, author of the highly successful and enjoyable, though somewhat shaky, *History of British Birds*, 1857, wrote letters to *The Times* encouraging people to put food out for the birds. But his request fell on fairly stony ground, since the thrifty Victorians didn't believe in admitting to waste of any kind, especially in the kitchen.

John Freeman Dovaston was probably the first man
to set up a bird table. Woodcut by Thomas Bewick.

In Germany, at about the same time, a wealthy landowner – the Baron von Berlepsch – was pioneering techniques of large-scale bird management. His primary interest was in the control of forest pests, but the aesthetics of bird encouragement played a significant part in his thinking. Despite the fact his main efforts went into the development of nestboxes for woodland species (as we shall see in chapter four) and that he underestimated the importance of food supply in relation to bird populations, he nevertheless experimented with the provision of artificial winter food supplies. His precise and demanding instructions for the erection and provision of 'food-houses' and 'food-bells' make fascinating reading. And he did much to encourage the spread of practical and unsentimental attitudes to the currently woolly world of bird preservation. His principal belief was that protection required an intimate knowledge of the birds' biology, and he held that man's excesses had to be balanced by providing natural or near-natural conditions – thus von Berlepsch made it his business to lay down most precise requirements for his experiments. While he may have been somewhat over-demanding, his thinking was decidedly in advance of his times . . . 'a thorough and rational protection of birds is only possible where the representatives of agriculture and forestry join forces with those who are interested in birds from aesthetic and ethical motives, and work together for a common good. Unfortunately much energy is wasted in angry quarrels.' That could as easily have been written today.

The Baron von Berlepsch designed special apparatus for preparing heated bird food. (See food tree on page 67)

It was the long hard winter of 1890 which softened the British heart and induced large-scale bird feeding, especially in cities. By 1910, according to *Punch*, bird feeding had become a national pastime and commercial interests had begun to offer special furniture. Possibly the first person to suffer financially from the practice was brought to court during the latter stages of the First World War, in the winter of 1916–17. Sophia Stuart was charged with wasting food, when a police sergeant found a quantity of bread cut into small pieces and scattered over the ground at front and back of the defendant's house in Woking. He solemnly collected half a pound as evidence and charged the unfortunate woman. Mrs Stuart, an elderly woman who had lost her only son, claimed 'the birds are my children, I have nothing else to love', and she stoutly informed the constable that she had fed the birds for years and proposed to continue. She claimed that she only used unclean crusts, and that it was not wasted if given to one's fellow creatures whether they went on two legs or four. In spite of her efforts, Mrs Stuart was found guilty and fined two pounds. I wonder how many people offered to pay her fine.

It would make an interesting exercise to work up a defence brief for Mrs Stuart, since she could have claimed that in feeding birds with scrap food she was working for the war effort. At any time, birds fulfil a vital role in the healthy functioning of our planet's system: as insect controllers, as agents of seed dispersal and, last but not least, as a primary food source. She should have claimed that she was ensuring the survival of useful allies!

Importance of winter feeding

Much has been made of the importance of winter bird feeding as a means of saving birds from extinction. but most of the evidence won't stand serious consideration. Bird numbers are primarily controlled by the availability of their natural foods; artificial feeding can have only a marginal influence. But it is an entirely worthwhile practice. Quite apart from the fact that it does have *some* practical effect, one reason for bird feeding is to use up kitchen scraps in a constructive manner. However, principally, the exercise gives us a lot of pleasure by attracting birds to a place where we see them to advantage. In really hard weather, extra feeding almost certainly saves a lot of individuals from an early grave. James Fisher, the ornithologist, estimated that a million birds survived the 1962–3 winter by courtesy of bird tables. Certainly feeding sustains a higher bird population in winter, at a time when the garden is at its least colourful, and that is a prime objective. Remember, though, that this sort of feeding is at best a substitute for natural food.

Sometimes people claim that feeding birds is wrong because it interferes with the natural course of events. But the fact is that we interfere in the lives of our fellow creatures and vegetation in almost everything we do, and much of this activity is entirely proper. In any case the provision of a measure of food and water, together with a few nestboxes, represents a modest return for the loss of natural habitat we have inflicted on our wild neighbours. Taken to its logical conclusion, the 'antis' should go round knocking down swallow and house-martin nests built under man's own roof in order to persuade these erring creatures to find themselves a more natural cliff or cave.

One thing is certain, if you do decide to feed the birds, the best time to do it is in winter. Having started, you are honour-bound to continue until the dark days are over and your artificially maintained population is able to fend for itself in the increasingly plentiful days of spring.

In cold weather birds face several problems. The ground may be so hard that they cannot get at the invertebrate creatures of the soil. Worms migrate downwards in dry or cold conditions; days are short, so hunting time is limited. Many blue tits, though, take advantage of street lights to work overtime and they forage almost without stopping in mid-winter. Provided the birds' plumage is in good condition they are perfectly able to withstand low temperatures, but inevitably their energy requirement is increased as

Pied wagtail in snow, conditions when insects are hard to find.

temperatures drop and they use fuel to keep warm. Many birds lose ten per cent or more of their body weight overnight in cold weather, and the short daylight hours must produce food to replace the lost fat. While a large bird like a gull may manage comfortably for a couple of days, provided it can fill its belly with a decent fish from the fish quay or some high-energy waste from a rubbish tip, a wren has a continuous appetite. Small species have a relatively larger-scale food requirement. Though physically small, they have a proportionately larger body surface and lose heat fast. Birds must maintain the highest body temperature of any animal – between 104°F and 112°F (40°C and 44.4°C), as against man's 98.6°F (37.0°C). And chemical reactions occur more rapidly at high temperatures. One way or another songbirds must work hard and fast at feeding.

Bird tables and their siting

Ground feeders, such as blackbirds, thrushes, dunnocks and moorhens prefer to feed at ground level, so they are best fed from a suitable tray which is taken in at night to cheat the rats. But put the tray a good 6 ft (1.8 m) from the sort of cover which might hide a stalking cat. The greatest variety of

Some birds feed at ground level, some are happier several feet up.

species, however, come to visit a bird tray which is fixed 5 ft (1.5 m) or so off the ground, in a position where most of them will merely regard it as an unusually shaped tree branch. Tits, finches and robins will be the regular visitors, making a dozen or so everyday customers. There is great potential, too, for surprises when using this kind of tray, as we shall see later, and a fair chance of colourful visitors arriving – like woodpeckers, nuthatches and exotic creatures from Scandinavia and the Mediterranean. Even if your only contact with the outside world is by way of a window above ground-floor level, you have a fighting chance of seducing birds to take advantage of your offerings, depending of course on the kind of greenery there is in the neighbourhood.

Bird tables may be erected on a post or hung from a branch or a bracket. The tray should offer a food surface of 1½ to 2 sq ft. Naturally, there should be no easy access for cats. Therefore, ideally, the post should be made from a piece of water pipe which will probably prove too slippery for them to climb; or perhaps the post can be sheathed in plastic tube which has the same effect. A rustic pole of the sort which is all too often on sale in garden shops and the like merely invites cats and other predators to shin up and take pot luck! The worst monstrosity on sale is the combination bird table and nestbox where any unfortunate owner of the nestbox is faced with an endless procession of callers, threatening his peace and causing territorial ructions.

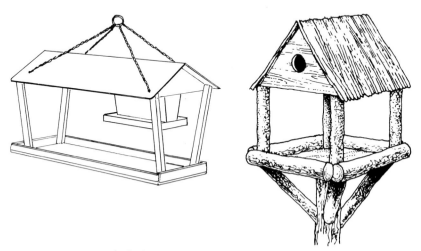

RSPB bird tables (left) are designed to please the birds.
Avoid versions (right) which invite trouble by
encouraging birds to nest over the dining room.

51

If possible, the table should be protected from hot sun and driving winds; a roof is not essential, but has the advantage that it may keep off the worst of the rain. Some ornamental bird tables have the luxury of a thatched roof, which at least offers sparrows some useful nest material. If you can have one of these, be careful it doesn't make access easier for squirrels and cats which may jump from a nearby vantage point and find the thatch offers a good landing grip.

The tray should be cleaned often, so it is important that the coaming which frames it has a few convenient gaps to allow odds and ends of crumbs to be swept away. Making a tray is easy enough. Kevin Baker illustrated a couple of suitable designs (see below and pages 51 and 54), but there is little doubt that the most practical bird table, offering good value for money, is the one sold by the RSPB (for address see page 181). Designed first and foremost from the point of view of the birds, it *works* well, and this is, after all, exactly what the human customer is looking for.

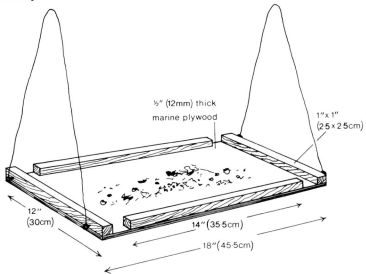

½″ (12mm) thick
marine plywood

1″ x 1″
(2.5 x 2.5cm)

12″
(30cm)

14″ (35.5cm)

18″ (45.5cm)

A simple bird table, which may be fixed on a post or hung from a tree.
Note the gaps in the coaming, allowing for easy cleaning.

If you make your own, check carefully that there are no sharp edges or protruding nails which might cut or damage the birds. Enclosing the feeding area with chicken wire will certainly keep starlings out, something which many people regard as desirable (not me!), but it has the undesirable effect of depriving access to thrushes, doves and woodpeckers. Probably the best solution is to provide food in a variety of ways, each allowing different birds

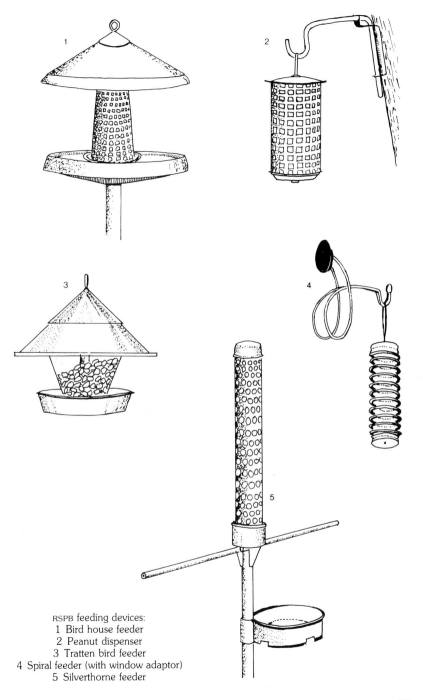

RSPB feeding devices:
1 Bird house feeder
2 Peanut dispenser
3 Tratten bird feeder
4 Spiral feeder (with window adaptor)
5 Silverthorne feeder

a chance to get a share of the offerings. The RSPB sell scrap cages, peanut baskets, seed globes and so on, and in no time at all you will start to devise your own fiendish contraptions for defeating sparrows and the dreaded starlings. One way of beating the starlings is to feed at first light, before they have had time to fly in from their overnight roosting place – which may be many miles away. Since birds lose weight overnight, this makes sense anyway, giving your residents a good start to the day.

House sparrows, like starlings, are not easy to outwit. They are omnivorous and they are a successful species by virtue of the very fact that they have specialised in living as mess mates with man. They are tough customers at the bird table, scattering food about in a tiresome manner and ousting all non-sparrow competition. Tending to operate in pugnacious gangs, they terrorise other small birds and take what they want by virtue of their aggressiveness and sheer numbers. Thrusting and showing their muscle, house sparrows sweep the dunnocks, chaffinches and tits out of the way. What can be done about this problem? Not much, but we may take advantage of one of their characteristics to give other species a short respite. They are cocky birds, and impudent – yet they are at the same time cautious

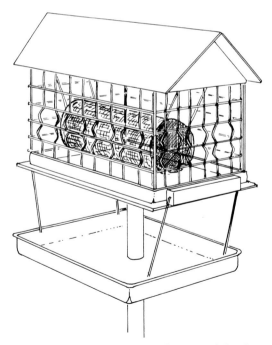

The Jamie Wood bird table has a caged section to foil starlings.

by nature, suspicious of anything new. So food placed in a different position may be left untouched for other birds to enjoy undisturbed for a while. Putting food in several different places may help too. A novel food basket or bag will be safe from their attention for a few days, though they will always win through in the end.

Not many years ago sparrows were foiled by hanging mesh baskets of the sort designed for the acrobatic tits, and much used by greenfinches. The sparrows showed interest in them and fluttered alongside ineffectively, but failed to get a grip on the mesh. Thus, they hung about to pick up any pieces of nut which fell to the ground. As the years went by they learnt to grasp the side of the basket and pick out the nuts in greenfinch fashion. Now this habit is widespread, another example of the learning ability so strikingly demonstrated by the blue tits when they found out how to open milk bottles. But house sparrows are versatile performers, taking seeds from seedheads in the manner of a goldfinch, working over trees like a woopecker and hawking for flying insects like a flycatcher – they are pretty well invincible.

The guiding principle for successful bird-table operation is to offer food in an enterprising variety of ways. If the feeding station ends up looking like a Christmas tree so much the better. Quite apart from the main dish offered on the table itself, there should be hanging baskets, seed hoppers, titbells and anything else you may think of. The object is to give as wide a range of foodstuffs in as wide a range of dishes as possible. Avoid collapsible or *bouncy* spiral wire feeders though, as they may trap a bird's leg while rebounding from the shock of its arrival.

The table then has been sited carefully to afford good all-round vision to its visitors, while being 6 ft (1.8 m) or so from convenient cover. Birds will make use of convenient staging posts on their way to and from the bird table, so ensure these are available. If there are no suitable branches, provide some substitutes in the form of posts or horizontal perches.

Varieties of food

Different birds have different food requirements and different search patterns for satisfying them. This is, after all, the main reason why they manage to coexist so successfully. Therefore, the shrewd bird gardener studies his potential bird list, and supplies and serves food accordingly. Some species are primarily vegetarian, some are seed-eaters, some are carnivorous and some like a bit of everything. If you take a look at a bird's foraging tools you will straight away have a fair idea of what it needs. Finches have nutcracker bills, adapted to crack and crush, and they feed mostly on grain and seeds. They are hard-billed. Robins and wrens have slender bills designed for the delicate process of probing for grubs, caterpillars and other insects. They are soft-billed. Hawks have hooked bills for tearing flesh. Gulls have general-purpose bills.

Different bill shapes are designed to deal
with different feeding preferences.
1 Wren.   2 Herring gull.   3 Greenfinch.   4 Peregrine.

Birds eat an astonishing variety of items when they are available, though by and large they do have a decided order of preference. Thrushes prefer the rich meat of worms, but will take snails or fruit as second best. Blackbirds search for worms in the first light of dawn, only later resorting to the bird table. Natural food is clearly the best for them, and if possible this is what should be provided on the bird table and the ground feeding tray. Rowan berries, elderberries, crab apples, hazel and almond nuts, boiled conkers, sweet chestnuts, acorns and beech mast are all highly suitable, though it will be more convenient for your guests if you crush, or chop and grate the harder nuts.

Thrushes will gladly take your fruit straight from the tree, but may well be diverted if you are able to offer rejected fruit collected from your local fruiterer. Squash it first, it will be much appreciated in cold weather. If you can go to the expense of buying commercially prepared food, then Haith's 'Songster Food' is a great success with blackbirds, robins and dunnocks (for address see page 181). And peanuts please almost every kind of bird. Kitchen scraps are not only taken by the obvious 'general purpose' birds like starlings but also by the specialist insect-eaters like blackcap, chiffchaff, tree creeper, and woodpeckers. And seed-eating birds like linnet, corn bunting, lesser redpoll, to say nothing of tawny owls and herons are also attracted. All these, and many others, have patronised well-stocked bird tables.

Suitable bird-table food

Animal fats, good for warblers, tits, robins, woodpeckers, nuthatches
Suet (beef best, or mutton)
Marrow bones, cracked.
Bacon rinds (short pieces)
Chicken carcass (try hanging it from a tree)
Tinned pet food
Mealworms
Maggots
Ants' eggs
Cheese
Hard-boiled egg

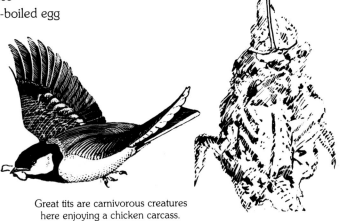

Great tits are carnivorous creatures here enjoying a chicken carcass.

Fruit, for thrushes, etc
Fresh, dried or decaying
Berries of all sorts

Nuts, of all sorts
Peanuts (not salted)
Almonds
Hazel
Brazils (for nuthatches, jam them in a tree crevice)

57

Seeds
Mixed (ie Swoop, from shops)
Hemp (a 'best buy' but must be kept dry – eagerly taken by greenfinches,
bullfinches and buntings, nuthatches, woodpeckers)
Canary (chaffinches)
Millet
Maize
Corn
Melon
Sunflower (heaven for greenfinches)

General
Boiled rice (not raw)
Potato (boiled or baked in jacket)
Stale cake crumbs
Coconut (in shell, *not* desiccated)
Uncooked pastry (tree creepers like it)
Biscuit crumbs
Bread-crumbs
Oats (coarse, but raw, not offered as porridge which is glutinous and sticks to
plumage and bills)

The list is almost endless, so try experimenting and remember that any left-over delicacies such as stilton rind, Christmas pudding or even haggis will be gratefully received. The only thing to avoid is salted or highly spiced or dehydrated foods. Make the offerings of either a size large enough to discourage birds from carrying it away to drop for the rats to find, or small enough to be eaten on the spot.

Bread is a controversial subject. Many people argue heatedly (and wrongly) that it should not be offered on bird tables. There are certainly dangers to be avoided. Dry bread may swell inside the bird's crop and choke it, so be careful to make it moist (sparrows, and others, are careful to dunk dry bread before eating it). One solution is to soak the crumbs in bacon grease, which will be appreciated. And here is the good news about white bread. According to Derek Goodwin of the Natural History Museum, London, the incidence of beri-beri in London's street pigeons has been all but eliminated since they have been enjoying the modern vitamin-enriched sliced bread. Make of that what you will. Eric Simms, the well-known broadcaster and writer on birds, compiled a list of the birds which he had seen taking bread in the outer suburbs of London, and they totalled twenty-three – including mallard; herring-, common black-headed and lesser black-backed gulls; feral pigeon; woodpigeon; carrion crow; jay; great, blue and coal tit; song thrush; blackbird; robin; dunnock; starling; skylark; greenfinch; chaffinch; siskin; house and tree sparrow. Doubtless more will join the list. At a popular bird-feeding place by a car park in a woodland area of Humberside, long-tailed tits joined the queue for white bread crumbs. I once enticed a wild whooper swan to come to a well-known brand of sliced white over a period of weeks. So there may be few surprises, but a lot of delights, in store for us all.

House sparrows dunk their dry bread
to make it more palatable.

Finches present something of a problem in that they prefer seeds. However, seeds are expensive and extraordinarily difficult to serve without scattering. If they are offered in a mixed variety then the birds will throw them all over the place as they search diligently for those they like best. They also need to be kept dry, of course. Seed hoppers are notoriously ineffective, but at last the RSPB has produced a globe feeder which works effectively. It is designed to dispense peanuts or bird-seed mixture of the 'Swoop' type, and is constructed in such a way that seed will flow from a generously sized reservoir down to a feeding point which is easily achieved by tits. This, so far, has defeated the wily sparrows. If you fill the feeder with peanuts because you want to attract greenfinches (and sparrows), then you must

59

devise a suitable perch which allows the finches to get a grip. Incidentally, this RSPB globe feeder provides the only really satisfactory way of offering hemp.

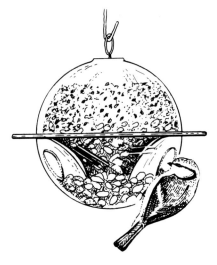

The RSPB globe feeder is ideal for offering seeds in bulk.

Peanuts are almost the perfect product for the dedicated feeder. Convenient to handle, store and serve, they are energy-packed with a high calorie content. But avoid mouldy nuts which have turned yellow at all costs, as they may be highly poisonous, producing aflatoxin, a toxin which kills the liver cells and has caused the death of many garden birds. Unshelled peanuts will be eaten by a variety of species in considerable quantity. Offered freely, they will be used up at the rate of several pounds a week, therefore it is best to present them in bags or cages which force the birds to work at the job of freeing them. Strung, in their shells, they provide innocent amusement for us as we watch the acrobatic tits breaking and entering. But be careful that you don't string them on multi-thread cotton which might tangle up their feet. If it suits them, tits may perch on the bird table to haul up a string of nuts 'bill over claw', a version of their natural behaviour whereby they pull leafy twigs closer to inspect them for caterpillars.

Tits and greenfinches are the prime customers for peanuts, but other species take advantage of the titbits which fall to the ground. Dunnocks, and on occasion bramblings, will forage below while as many as three species of tit and greenfinches are working above. Robins are fond of peanuts, too, and although they find great difficulty in fluttering alongside

Siskins eat spruce and pine seeds, but have taken
enthusiastically to peanuts, high calorie food which
has fuelled their range expansion.

and grabbing a morsel, they can manage it. Jays, chaffinches and, indeed, bramblings, have all learnt to enjoy the bounty of the bag. One of the most remarkable instances of a bird expanding its range through a liking for peanuts is that of the siskin, a small acrobatic finch more closely associated with Forestry Commission conifer plantations, where they enjoy spruce and pine seeds in spring and summer. Originally confined to the Caledonian pine forest of Scotland, they slowly extended south from the mid-nineteenth century, colonising parkland and conifer forests and reaching North Wales, Norfolk and the New Forest a hundred years later. Then, some twenty years ago, they started to come into gardens and feed on peanuts in south-east England. The habit has now spread through most of the country and the numbers wintering have increased, till nowadays we see them feeding on tideline seed debris on the Exe Estuary in Devon, for example. They displayed a curious preference for peanuts offered in the small red plastic netting containers used by greengrocers for packing carrots, coming readily to gardens which hung these bags rather than the conventional RSPB scrap cage. And furthermore, it was confidently asserted that they preferred these red mesh bags to any other device. These birds are not only from the increasing British breeding population, but also from Scandinavia and the

Baltic. The numbers fluctuate widely from year to year, but are generally at their highest in March and early April just before the birds migrate back to their breeding grounds – either in northern Britain or across the North Sea. Those winters when few siskins are seen probably coincide with good seed crops nearer to their breeding grounds.

Tits are the family which give the greatest pleasure to house-bound birdwatchers who simply enjoy the company of their birds. Their acrobatics are always a joy to watch, and they display a touching enthusiasm for any feeding device which offers nuts or fat. They very much enjoy coconut, which should be put out fresh, in the shell. Just saw the nut in half and suspend it so that the rain doesn't spoil the flesh. Never offer coconut in desiccated or ground forms, as the food swells inside the stomach with dire results. This is especially true in the breeding season, when juvenile tits will not survive the treatment.

Blue tits search leafy trees for caterpillars;
they find it easy to attack a coconut from underneath.

Once the raw coconut has been eaten away, the remaining shell will serve as a container for various forms of bird pudding. Fill with kitchen scraps and top up with hot fat, then leave overnight so that the mixture sets. When more or less solid, stick in a suitable twig to serve as a perch and turn it back again to hang from a tree branch, or from the bird table. The pudding will last a fair time, providing high-energy food for the tits and a lot of pickings for the ground feeders which forage underneath.

Scrap baskets, such as the standard RSPB wire cage, are useful because they can be filled indoors at your convenience and the food doesn't get scattered about quite so freely as with the bird table. But, like the peanut bags, only certain birds will be able to feed from them. Thus, it is important to spread your largesse by way of a variety of feeding stations and devices.

Suet is another high-energy food, and it melts down well for titbell use. The short variety is more appropriate than the stringy and it serves as an acceptable substitute for the fat grubs and insects which woodpeckers enjoy. Stuffed into mesh bags, or scrap baskets, or stuck into crevices and crannies on tree trunks, it will act as a magnet for colourful birds like great spotted woodpeckers and welcome visitors like long-tailed tits. The brilliantly coloured woodpeckers are relatively recent bird-table addicts, having first taken to the practice some time in the late 1950s. Now they are common visitors to feeding stations. Incidentally, like tree creepers they are fond of uncooked pastry. If you daub suet into the crevices of an old, gnarled Scots pine, it will attract other visitors as well as the woodpeckers and tree creepers – for instance, goldcrests and even firecrests, together with wintering chiffchaffs and blackcaps.

Lastly, after that catalogue of feasting, it may be worth putting out a small quantity of grit – fine sand, gravel or even small bits of coal – to aid the avian digestion process. It makes sense to provide a small amount on, or under, the bird table.

Don't be discouraged if, after all your efforts, birds don't flock to your feast. It takes them time to adjust to a new feeding opportunity, as you will find if you move a familiar device, or paint something a new colour. Or perhaps there is a welcome abundance of natural food nearby, which will of course be more attractive, nutritious and generally health-promoting than anything you may have provided.

It is important to keep a bird table clean because there is an ever-present danger of bacterial infection from bird droppings. And do not allow a pile of uneaten, unwanted food to accumulate. Move the table once or twice in a winter season to discourage a build-up of the potentially dangerous droppings. And a warning – don't overfeed your birds. It doesn't make sense to provide great mounds of food, attracting quantities of birds and increasing the risk of salmonellosis and tuberculosis, both of which are common bacterial infections in wild birds. The object should be to provide a welcome *supplement,* but not so much as to induce dependence on bird table food at the expense of active foraging for a diversity of wild seeds, grasses and insects in a natural manner.

Feeding times

It is probably best to feed at regular times, morning or late afternoon, for instance, or, better still, first thing in the morning only. And, at the risk of being accused of tiresome repetition, I must emphasise that, having started putting out food as winter approaches, it is most important that you should continue. If you suddenly stop feeding, your happy band of pensioners will suffer greatly. So, if you have to go away be sure to leave freshly filled titbells and seed hoppers which will keep them occupied until your return.

There has been much controversy about the advisability of putting out bird-table food during the breeding season. And while it is perfectly true that adult birds are capable of making an intelligent choice for themselves about food times, it is equally true that artificial food has killed many nestlings. Seed-eating birds, like chaffinches, feed their young by regurgitation on a

Juvenile chaffinches begging for choice caterpillars.

mix which consists largely of insects with a certain amount of vegetable material. But they take a few sips of water, and the method of feeding ensures that the young are not fed hard, indigestible mouthfuls. The young chaffinches, which will soon learn to feed themselves on seeds, are at first fed caterpillars by their parents. There is a real danger that juvenile birds may get stuffed with unsuitable food. A stomach full of peanuts, for example, is disastrous for a nestling blue tit. And a full payload of bread scraps, deficient in protein for the growing youngster, will stunt growth.

The commercially produced soft-bill food is perhaps the most suitable offering in spring and summer, if you want to keep feeding, since this is effectively a substitute for live insects. At this time of year it makes sense to provide baked and crushed eggshells which are a convenient source of additional calcium.

In the breeding season you can also stuff the peanut cages and scrap baskets with straw and feathers, dog or cat combings, short bits of cotton and bits of cotton-wool. These will be welcomed and taken for nest material.

Recipes

1 Cakes and puddings for the bird table

EDWIN COHEN'S PUDDING

8 oz (200 g) beef suet, 12 oz (300 g) coarse oatmeal, 2–3 oz (50–75 g) flour, 5 oz (125 g) water
Mix flour and oatmeal with liquid fat and water to stiff paste. Bake in shallow pie dish to form flat cake at 175°C for approximately one hour.

MISS TURNER'S MAIZE CAKE

Mix 3 oz maize meal in a bowl with equal quantities of chopped nuts, hemp, canary and millet seed. Stir with boiling water till coagulated, and add two beaten eggs. Tie tightly in a cloth and bake at 175°C for fifty minutes to one hour.

TIM'S BIRD CAKE

2 lb (1 kg) self-raising flour, 8 oz (200 g) margarine, a little sugar
Mix with water and bake like a rock bun.

ANTI-SPARROW PUDDING

Boil together one cup of sugar and one cup of water for five minutes. Mix with one cup of melted fat (suet, bacon or ordinary shortening), and leave it to cool. Then mix with bread-crumbs, flour, bird seed, a little boiled rice and scraps, until the mixture is very stiff. Pack into any kind of tin can or glass jar. Lay the can on its side in a tree, on the window sill, or any place where birds can perch and pick out the food. The can must be placed securely so that the birds cannot dislodge it, nor rain get inside. May not fool sparrows for long, though, so don't take it too seriously.

2 Fillings for bird bells, suet sticks and pine cones

BASIC TITBELL RECIPE

Fill the upturned bell with seeds, peanuts, cheese, oatmeal, sultanas, cake crumbs and other scraps. Pour in hot fat to the brim. Insert a short piece of twig into the mix to act as a learner's perch, if necessary. Leave to harden. Turn the bell over and hang in a suitable place where small birds like blue tits are already accustomed to come for food.

PINE CONE SURPRISE

Leave a large fir cone near a fire or radiator for several days so that it opens its scales. Gather the seeds to include in the mix. Take beef suet with any meat or fat trimmings. Melt it, stir in cake crumbs, hemp, millet seed, raisins, the pine-cone seeds, and anything else you think the birds might fancy. Pour the hot mix onto an opened cone, or dip the cone in, then allow to cool. Or stuff the holes of a feeding stick with the cooled mixture. Fix the cone or stick amongst the branches of a tree or tree substitute.

Great spotted woodpecker enjoying a pine cone surprise.

THE BARON VON BERLEPSCH FOOD-TREE RECIPE

This mix was formulated by the good Baron as a means of extending the plenteous times of summer to woodland birds in winter, and provides high-energy, intensive feeding. It was to be poured, hot, onto either the branches of a live young conifer or an imitation tree made of separate branches. Since living trees promptly lost their leaves – the needles – when hot fluids were

Baron von Berlepsch food tree.

poured on them, he recommended this practice only in the sort of wood-lands which could suffer the sight of an ugly and diseased tree. In more sensitive areas, he suggested using a felled tree, imported for the purpose. While still enjoying the Baron's recipes a century later, I think we may take it for granted that the birds will not fuss too much over the method of presentation, and this recipe serves well as a bird-bell mix. The Baron tells us that it is by no means necessary to keep closely to the ingredients; it is only to serve as a guide, though the chief part of the mix should always consist of hemp. These are:

5 oz (125 g) breadcrumbs
3 oz (75 g) hemp seed, whole or crushed
3 oz (75 g) millet seeds
1½ oz (23 g) sunflower seeds
1½ oz (23 g) oats
2 oz (30 g) ants' eggs
1½ oz (23 g) dried elderberries
Suet (beef suet), the less stringy the better

Mix well, fill the bell and bind with hot, melted suet. Cool. Add more suet, melt and cool again. The second time of cooling produces a harder consis-tency. This mix offers a meal of high calorific value to birds which have difficulty in finding their preferred insect diet in winter.

Another titbell mix, equally suitable for open offer on the bird table:
This comprises seeds, peanuts, oatmeal, cake crumbs and cheese. Put them in a container (bird bell, baking dish), pour hot fat to cover. Leave to set. In the case of an open tray, simply turn it out onto the bird table. Bacon or sausage fat is ideal, using 8 oz (200 g) of melted fat to 1 lb (500 g) of mix, very roughly.

3 Mealworm culture (robins will thank you for your efforts)

Take a smooth-sided container such as a large circular biscuit tin or one of those out-dated and highly unsuitable glass bowls traditionally used for unfortunate goldfish. An open top provides plenty of air, but have a wire mesh lid which will foil escape attempts.

Put a 4 in to 6 in (10 cm to 15 cm) layer of dry wheat bran or barley meal in the bottom. Now a layer of hessian sacking. Add a vegetable layer of carrot, turnip, banana and apple skins, dry bread, raw potato, cabbage, as available – but ensure that the medium does not become too wet as it will

Coal (left) and great tits feeding from tit bell.

then ferment, smell appalling and probably kill the mealworms. A good productive mixture will not smell. Then take more hessian sacking and add more vegetable/bran layers to produce a multi-tier sandwich of mealworm delight. Introduce 200–300 mealworms (mealworms from an aviculturist's pet shop, *not* a fishing shop's maggots) and keep in a warm room.

After a few weeks the mealworms, fat and happy, will turn into creamy pupae, then into little black beetles, which represent your breeding stock. They lay eggs which hatch into mealworms, and so on. Crop the mealworms in accordance with all the scientific principles of MSY (maximum sustainable yield). If you want to start an empire, prepare other tins and prime them with a few bits of dry bread from an existing colony. These will carry beetle eggs.

69

Robins are very fond of mealworms, provide them and
you will soon have a bird which feeds from your hand.

4 Earthworm culture

Earthworms, *Lumbricus terrestris*, are bisexual, each individual exhibiting
both male and female characteristics. But it still needs two to start a family.
Use a suitable box in a shady position. Fill with a mixture of sand, well-
ground manure (which may include a generous helping of household
peelings and greens), rich loamy soil and peat moss in equal parts. Water
and mix well. Turn and sprinkle with yet more water every few days.
Introduce your breeding stock after two weeks, when the mix has cooled to
between 66°F and 75°F (19°C and 24°C). In three months you will have a
powerhouse of worm production, to be culled for your ground-feeders'
tray.

THREE
Birding from
the kitchen window

Establishing a hierarchy

A well-found bird table will be a delight to watch, especially in winter when it is fulfilling its purpose. A continuous stream of finches and tits will share the pickings with starlings, sparrows and perhaps even woodpeckers and nuthatches. There will be much interest in putting names to the birds, in sorting out their plumages, and in watching the spotty juveniles adopt their adult flying suits. But there will also be interest in watching behaviour at the bird table. Some species will appear tolerant of all-comers, some will object strongly – even to the company of their own kind. Both robins and blackbirds, for instance, may hold their breeding territories through the winter, and do not encourage trespass. Blue tits and greenfinches, by contrast, enjoy a daily round where they may visit a whole series of different gardens. There is a suggestion that some great tits are developing a tendency to sit tight in garden territories, possibly encouraged by the very availability of bird table food.

Starling and blue tit
engaging in a bird table quarrel.

Study the behaviour of your breakfast guests over a period of time, and you should be able to work out a pecking order. Birds are easily inclined to quarrel over their food, and these feeding squabbles are well observed at the bird table, where they inevitably come into close contact. One threatens another by posturing ie gaping aggressively, spreading wings and tail. It is largely a game of bluff, since neither individual wants to come to blows, wasting energy and risking the loss of precious feathers, to say nothing of the danger from predators if they aren't keeping a proper watch. But the game has a serious object, because the winner gets the choicest titbit (and at other times, the best perch, the best breeding territory and the most desirable mate). So the establishment of a pecking order is a meaningful affair, and it plays a real part in everyday bird life, to say nothing of our own.

The peck order, or, more scientifically, dominance hierarchy, is so called because the experimental work which demonstrated its validity was carried out with domestic hens. They establish dominance by pecking about the head and shoulders of rivals. It applies to species which live social or colonial lives, involving a great deal of shoulder-rubbing with other birds, not necessarily of their own species. The process involves fights, bickering and bluff which continues until an order emerges. From the boss bird down-wards, everyone knows his place, though bickering is constant, with individuals jostling and 'trying it on' with the object of improving their rating. The dominant cock has it all his own way, eating the best food and fathering the most chicks on the most attractive hens. He therefore leads an aggressive life, defending and consolidating his position till he is inevitably toppled as age creeps up on him. In a mixed flock there will still be a peck order, which explains why the greedy starlings take precedence at the bird table, followed in the hierarchy by house sparrows, great, blue, marsh or willow and coal tits in that order. In fact blue tits will rob great tits almost as often as they are robbed by them, but without a doubt these two species dominate the other tits, with coal tits decidedly the weakest in the hierarchy.

Blackbirds fight enthusiastically among themselves, with a great deal of noisy chasing across the lawn and through the shrubbery. As a species they dominate song thrushes, taking earthworms from their beaks and waiting till they crack the meat out of snail shells before moving in to steal it. If you are lucky enough to have a resident mistle thrush, he will dominate both blackbirds and song thrushes! Starlings are aggressive and quarrelsome by nature; it is one of the traits which has led them to success, in population terms at least if not in terms of our approbation. This can be seen as they work over a garden lawn, but is most obvious at the bird table, where

Song thrushes have developed the technique for breaking snail shells,
but the more aggressive blackbirds sometimes enjoy the reward.

the constraints of space and the stimulus of abundant food work them up to
fever pitch. Working fast, they grab the biggest bits and, in their anxiety to fill
up and get away from a potentially dangerous situation, they scatter food far
and wide. In early spring, the sexes are easily distinguishable, the males
having blue-grey at the base of the bill where females show pink. Armed
with this knowledge you will soon see that the males are the ones feeding on
plenty at the bird table, while the submissive females are banished to less
attractive places.

Predators

One of the advantages of communal activities, as practised by starlings, is
that there is safety in numbers, and predators are less likely to take advantage of surprise where many are feeding. For birds have good reason to be
apprehensive while foraging at the bird table: however carefully you have
sited it, and however effectively you have protected them from land-based
predators like cats and weasels, they are at risk from potent and persistent
enemies, airborne raptors belonging to their own class – owls and hawks.

When there is a sudden hush in your garden, with the small birds dashing
to disperse in cover, calling only the sharp cries of alarm, there is a predator
about. And the small birds are well able to recognise their enemies. A robin
will cringe when a sparrowhawk passes, but take no notice at all if a goose
flies by. There is good reason for alarm, and the necessary information is

programmed into the robin at birth. This innate knowledge tells which creatures to ignore and which to run away from, information which is the result of a lesson learnt long ago. Doubtless, the immediate experience of seeing one of your kind killed reinforces the understanding in a powerful manner. And, seeing the encounter from the other viewpoint, it is equally true that the sparrowhawk carries programmed information about suitable prey species. He has a built-in 'search image' which may encourage him to specialise in blue tits because instinct tells him that blue tits are for catching. And sparrowhawks are very efficient at catching small birds. It has been shown that they may take two-and-a-half per cent of a whole chaffinch population in the month of May.

The raptors are well designed for their job as hunter-killers. Sparrowhawks have broad, rounded wings by comparison with the more open-country falcons like peregrines, which have been designed for speed. But sparrowhawks work in amongst the trees and hedgerows, and while they enjoy a fair turn of speed they are also able to engage in fast turns and complicated manoeuvres, a useful facility if you're chasing a wildly jinking small bird. Like the other birds of prey, they are able to turn their fourth toe so that it is pointing backwards, allowing a tight grip with two sharp-clawed toes on either side of the victim's body. And the forward component of the

Sparrowhawks may visit the bird table
in search of their dinner too.

impact motion as they land on a victim causes the claws to lock automatically and grip fast, a sinister variation on the same mechanism which locks songbirds' feet to their roosting perch when they go to sleep. The bird must make a conscious effort to release its victim.

Sparrowhawks are not the only hunters which enjoy the living bounty of the bird table. Kestrels commonly take house sparrows and young starlings when they get the chance, behaviour that has been most observed in London, where they are now well established as breeding birds. Voles are their preferred diet, and they find good hunting along railway embankments, but if small mammals are scarce they will take many birds, and a bird table will become more interesting to them. Perhaps more surprisingly, there are records of kestrels coming to take broken dog biscuits and uncooked bacon rind from an Edinburgh bird table in a cold winter. The fact is that birds like sparrowhawks and kestrels are increasingly becoming aware of the potential offered by the bird feeding stations. No fewer than eight species have been recorded at their dirty work. Apart from those already mentioned there have been reports of tawny, barn and little owls; merlins; buzzards; and, astonishingly, goshawks. The goshawk was seen taking small birds from a bird table in a Yorkshire garden which adjoined a forestry plantation – typical habitat.

However disconcerting and, perhaps, upsetting it may be to see your garden birds carried off struggling by a predator, it is a perfectly natural everyday event in the bird world. Certainly it is not our responsibility to try to put an end to this hunting by controlling predators, which was the automatic, albeit ignorant, reaction of gamekeepers in the days when they held the view that anything which ate their precious charges must be doing harm. (It would also be naïve to think that all present-day gamekeepers have seen the light, but there is some evidence that a large proportion of them have!) To begin with, the predator is not as all-powerful as he is sometimes seen; he doesn't kill every time and, indeed, once he is unmasked he is molested by the very birds he is seeking. Blackbirds chivvy cats, rooks chivvy buzzards and songbirds gather to chivvy owls the moment they reveal themselves. This mobbing is a form of display, the birds most at risk banding together to draw attention to the danger. Hoping to avert attack, they feel there is some safety in numbers.

It then follows that the prey taken by a predator is going to represent the slowest/dimmest/weakest/most disabled of its stock, and therefore the stock is improved by this weeding out of less healthy individuals which might have bred and passed on their weakness. Finally, it is generally accepted that it is not in the predator's long-term interest to reduce its prey species. For example, the sparrowhawk has a special interest in ensuring there will be an abundance of sparrows for its progeny to chase. There is a nice parallel here with the behaviour of the fox hunting fraternity who, however often they may say they are trying to exterminate foxes, are in fact concerned to conserve their numbers in a comfortable balance so that there will always be enough to chase.

Thus, there is no sense in taking the law into your own hands and shooting or trapping predators – it doesn't serve the interests of the prey. Other potential natural enemies will step in to take advantage of the available surplus, or disease or parasites or shortage of food will perform the predator's task instead. And there are always far fewer predators than the animals on which they feed. Songbirds need only a relatively small patch of land to supply their needs, but a hawk or an owl needs a hunting territory which will run to dozens of acres. Insects are always more numerous than the shrews which eat them, and shrews are always more common than the owls which in turn eat *them* – a demonstrable concept which is known as the 'pyramid of numbers', where the so-called 'higher' animals come out on top. In essence an effective check is kept on the predator's population, in that it can only survive in relation to a higher population of its preferred prey species.

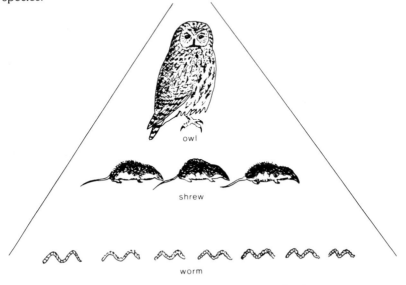

owl

shrew

worm

The pyramid of numbers. Our planet supports a lot of worms
which in turn support fewer shrews and even fewer owls.

Sadly the vision of a paradise garden where all is happiness and serenity is an unacceptable concept to the biologist. Predators, whether sparrowhawk or beetle, will do their thing and make their presence known. But it is all a question of attitude, and surely we should glory in the knowledge that their function is a totally healthy one. They leave the garden a stronger place than they found it. And their method of control is far preferable to the sort that comes from a poison or preparation bought at the garden centre.

Unusual garden visitors

One of the pleasures of bird table watching is the slow but steady way in which more and more species are being lured to join in. Not only kestrels and goshawks, fortunately, but more and more of the birds which formerly kept us at some distance. Great spotted woodpeckers and long-tailed tits are much commoner visitors than they once were. Goldcrests, firecrests, cirl buntings, woodcock, common snipe, water rail, kingfishers and dipper – all are species which have taken to the habit. Bearded tits have been encouraged to visit seed piles near reed beds at the Minsmere RSPB reserve. Little gulls have taken food scraps from a litter bin. It seems there is no limit to the possibilities.

Where you live will, of course, have a considerable bearing on your potential bird list. Sailors at sea have operated bird feeding stations for many years. On migration, many land birds have sought respite on weather ships and oil rigs, as well as ships steaming at sea. Kestrels which visited a weather ship at station India stayed three days and were fed on steak. A little auk was once desperate enough to take tinned sardines; bramblings and snow buntings, at 71° and 74° North respectively, enjoyed 'Swoop'. A great blue heron landed on the flight deck of HMS *Hermes*, of Falklands fame, when she was 500 miles east of Puerto Rico in the Caribbean, and was entertained on the quarterdeck for two days with dishes of pilchards. The cargo vessel *Sugar Crystal* was joined 140 miles south-west of Ireland, while on passage to Felixstowe, by thirty-four jackdaws and three rooks, which squabbled over grain spillage on the decks. On a more everyday level, no cross-Channel yachtsman can have failed to have the company, at some time or another, of a tired racing pigeon looking for a rest and some sustenance.

Great rarities have first revealed themselves on the bird table. In the severe winter of 1954–5, while there was thick snow on the ground, an unfortunate American warbler, which had found itself in England after an unscheduled Atlantic crossing, showed up on a south Devon bird table. This

Large numbers of birds—starlings in this case—take advantage
of the roosting facilities on oil rigs at migration time.

myrtle warbler, the first record for Britain, established itself in vigorous ownership of the food supply, seeing off the resident blue tits and even going so far as to deprive one of a feather, a considerable loss to a small bird in such freezing conditions. The warbler displayed a keen interest in bread and marmalade, thus causing some of us to suggest that it came from Peru to look for Paddington Bear.

The first record of a red-throated thrush, *Turdus ruficollis*, to be seen in Britain was made in a north Buckinghamshire urban garden in the winter of 1978–9. A Siberian species, this one was looked at with a certain amount of suspicion since it seemed highly possible it was an escaped cage bird. In the same way it would be unwise to assume that the budgerigars spotted on some bird tables had flown in from Wagga Wagga, Australia.

Nevertheless, rarities and reluctant arrivals aside, there are long-term trends to be discerned by studying the bird table. Great spotted woodpeckers and long-tailed tits appear to have come to stay, and the relatively recent colonisation of our islands by collared doves has been made easier by the freely available supply of food. Sparrowhawks and kestrels will presumably take to bird-table visiting in increasing numbers.

Not surprisingly, crows have learnt the advantages of artificial food. Magpies too, as part of a general increase in numbers, have become more common in country gardens as well as the suburbs, where there is a scarcity of gamekeepers. First they took the songbirds' eggs and young, and then moved in to take the food provided for them. Though it may be something of a strain for the bird enthusiasts to see magpies culling his hard-won neighbours, one just has to sit back and let them act as healthy predators and sort things out amongst themselves.

Jays will collect unshelled peanuts and carry them off for burying and subsequent digging up as a food store, in the same way that they bury vast numbers of acorns in autumn. This food storage is typical of other species such as nuthatches and tits, which hide food at a time when it is abundant, though it is particularly widespread amongst the crow family. It occurs when there is more food about than the birds are able to eat, and quite apart from obviously suitable items like nuts, they will hide bread or cheese pieces. This

Jays collect large numbers of acorns in autumn.

79

family propensity to store food gave rise to the 'thieving magpie' legend. And while wild birds do not carry off gold rings and diamond necklaces, it is highly likely that tame ones might do so when they are deprived of their natural foraging.

Winter feeders

Birds derive advantage from the autumn plenty by putting on fat and, as we have discussed in some cases, by laying up a winter store. It is at this time of year, when berries and seeds are plentiful, that you are at least likely to have a well attended bird table – the natural food available is a greater attraction. But it may be that your bird table is not particularly successful in a winter which follows a bumper seeding season. In other words, there is no substitute for natural food, and birds will prefer it given a choice. As well as seeds, there will still be a measure of life-support in the hibernating flies, spiders, woodlice, centipedes and so on, which find just enough warmth to overwinter in the fallen leaves of undergrowth. One of the characteristic sounds of winter is the crunching noise made by blackbirds as they thunder about in the shrubbery, foraging.

It is in hard weather, when the extreme cold requires more energy output by birds to maintain their body temperatures, that the bird table is a life-saver. The most obvious effect of the arrival of a cold snap is that more species will come for the food. There will be mistle thrushes, greenfinches, long-tailed tits, and more blackbirds. Fieldfares and redwings will visit the garden lawn and the bird table, and there will be bramblings feeding under the nut bags for fallen morsels. In extreme conditions, even the fiercely territorial robins will feed side by side. Other species will find their way in from exposed country to enjoy the relative shelter, including reed buntings and yellowhammers, grey wagtails, skylarks and meadow pipits, pheasants and moorhens. Wrens may take crumbs from bird tables in a way that is entirely untypical.

It is perhaps true that the existence of bird table food has made it possible for some normally migrant birds to stay with us and stick out our British winter. Blackcaps, which are overwintering in increasing numbers, mostly in the mild south and south-west, are particularly vulnerable to severe winters. They rely heavily on berries, such as those of *Cotoneaster* and honeysuckle, will eat the holly berries which are not exactly popular generally, and turn to ivy berries during the early spring as their preferred food. Rotting windfall apples are also important to them, and they have even been seen to take

Cotoneaster berries are an important winter
food source for those blackcaps which don't migrate.

mistletoe berries, a fruit which seems of little interest to most birds apart from
thrushes. It is in hard weather that blackcaps are most likely to be seen at
bird tables, looking for cake crumbs, fat, nuts and seeds, and this is the time
when a tray of rejected fruit from the shop will be most welcome. Overwintering chiffchaffs will come to the bird table, too, for crumbs and suet.

It is possible that bird-table offerings have fuelled the range expansion of
an exotic invader, the ring-necked parakeet. This attractive looking parrot,
originating from Africa and India, escaped from captivity, or was perhaps
deliberately released in some numbers (as a human response to its unre-
warding behaviour in captivity), at the end of the 1960s. Since then, starting
from a nucleus in the London suburbs and Kent, it has slowly but surely
colonised the south-east and established itself as a feral species and something of a pest. Omnivorous by nature, it prefers fruit and has a devastating
effect on apple orchards with its tendency to take just a couple of pecks at

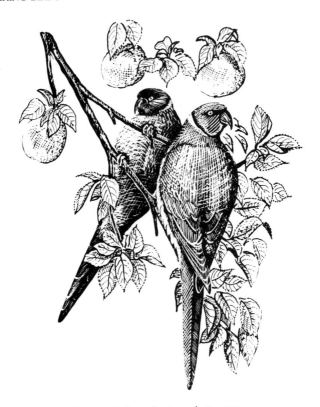

Ring-necked parakeets are fruit-eaters.

each fruit. It comes freely to bird tables and, breeding in tree holes, will presumably take to nestboxes. Even the most severe winters have failed to halt its spread, in spite of knowledgeable predictions that it could not survive the cold. Broadly speaking, it is true that birds are perfectly able to withstand the lowest temperatures, provided they are well fed and protected by healthy plumage.

In extreme winter conditions, when water is frozen and mudflats glazed by ice, water birds and waders suffer greatly. Herons and kingfishers must go down to the sea to find open water; pied wagtails cannot find their ditch-side insects; thrushes and robins cannot penetrate the frozen earth. And small birds like long-tailed tits, wrens and goldcrests may die because there aren't enough feeding hours in the day for them to meet their high energy requirements. So, once you start operating a winter bird table, it is of the utmost importance that you keep it well supplied through the dark months until April.

FOUR
Nests, nesting places and birds in boxes

History of nestboxes

Pigeon houses

Man-made nest sites have a long history, and originally their purpose was almost entirely in connection with the food potential of the species involved. It seems likely that pigeons were the first birds to be domesticated, by way of artificial nesting ledges which encouraged truly wild birds to breed in places where the keeper could harvest his share of the fat squabs. Pigeons were ideal candidates for domestication, with undemanding food requirements, an easily satisfied specification for nesting places, an easy-going disposition and tolerance of man. Above all, they had the astonishing ability to rear as many as ten clutches in a year, nourishing a pair of well-grown squabs while they incubated the next pair of eggs in the production line.

The pigeon technique for feeding young, even in the depths of winter, relies on their ability to produce 'pigeon's milk' from their crops. The formation of this milk is controlled by a hormone, prolactin, which is produced by both cock and hen in the last days of incubation. Thus, they are ready to ensure a protein supply to the newly hatched chicks for the first few days, till they are strong enough to eat at least a little solid food. The milk is secreted from the lining of the parent's crop, which thickens and, at hatching time, breaks off into cheesy curd. The parent takes the newly hatched squab's bill into its mouth, the squab automatically reaches in, and the parent regurgitates. After a few days the milk is supplemented with choice pieces of soft food or seeds. As time goes by the ratio changes, by hormonal cueing, so that the young get less and less milk.

Probably the first of these birds to be domesticated was in the Eastern Mediterranean. There are images of the pigeon in art dating back to 3100 BC, and certainly the birds were used as a source of food in Egypt before 2600 BC. In early cultures pigeons were sacred birds, associated with

Young pigeons are fed on 'milk', which is
regurgitated from the parent's crop.

Astarte, the goddess of fertility and fruitfulness. In India, as birds sacred to
the Hindu religion, they were allowed to colonise buildings and temples
without hindrance and without being exploited for food. In Classical Greece
they were associated with Aphrodite, as love symbols. The Romans linked
pigeons with Venus in the same way, but prudently took advantage of their
culinary qualities, as well as using them for messengers. Indeed, as Pliny the
Elder (AD 23–70) wrote in *Natural History*: 'Many persons have quite a
mania for pigeons – building towers for them on the top of their roofs, and
taking pleasure in relating the pedigree and noble origin of each'.

As enthusiastic pigeon fanciers, the Romans must have built pigeon cities,
or columbaria as they were known, in England. Whether the Saxons did so
is not clear, but the word 'cote' refers in part to a bird house, and 'culver',
though less widespread, probably refers to the wood pigeon and gave rise to
'culver house'. 'Doocot' is clear enough in its meaning and, indeed, the

Scots have cultured pigeons for a very long time. Near the coastal village of Wemyss, in Fife, there are two caves with dozens of man-made ledges cut out of the walls and the artificially enlarged roof, clearly designed to encourage rock pigeons. Carvings on the walls date back to the early Bronze Age, but are mainly Pictish (AD 400–900). Sadly, the archaeologists are as yet unable to date the ledges, so we cannot say whether the Picts farmed the pigeons or whether the practice was first associated with the later development of the nearby fourteenth-century castles of Wemyss and Macduff.

More widespread rearing of semi-domesticated pigeons for fresh meat, especially in winter, began in Britain with the Norman invasion, when the conquerors introduced the science of the 'colombier'. No twelfth-century castle was complete without its rows of pigeon holes, carefully built into a turret or high place, sheltered and south facing. with the enormous advantage that the birds foraged far and wide for their own food and did not require sustenance from a besieged garrison's meagre supplies. Soon the gentle pigeon became associated with warlike places, the substantial stone-built dovecot being an important part of any manor house or monastery.

On the wild Gower coast of South Wales, a natural cliff fissure was enclosed at some time in the thirteenth or fourteenth century to form a hollow pigeon buttress, known as the 'culver hole'. There were ramps giving access for the keeper, and three elegant slits making entrances for the birds – yet another arrangement designed to tempt wild rock pigeons to nest so that the occupants of a nearby castle could take a proportion of the squabs. The culver hole was rebuilt in the fifteenth century and still stands today, an astonishing structure which reminds us of the one-time importance of pigeon culture.

By the late thirteenth century a medieval bishop on his travels would expect a high standard of victualling, the dinner table liberally provided with bird meat. On tour, his chaplain would record disboursements for wine, beer, beef and so on. One note tells of His Lordship's purchase of '2 carcasses of beef, 9s 4d, 25 geese 5s 2½d, 24 pigeons 8d'. So along with the fish pond and the rabbit warren and the duck decoy, the dovecot was an important item in medieval animal architecture. Conradus Heresbachius, in his *Husbandrie*, 1577, wrote 'it behoveth especially to have good care for breeding of pigeons, as well for the great commoditie they yeelde to the kitchin, as for the profit and yearely revenue that they yeelde (if there be good store of corne seedes) in the market'.

The pigeon house was always carefully sited, to provide protection from prevailing winds. The Norman design involved a circular building, solidly planted on the ground with walls 3 ft (1 m) thick (no windows), gradually tapering, at the very top of the roof, to a 'lantern', which gave entrance for the birds. A single door at ground level allowed entrance for the pigeon keeper. Inside, the walls were covered with row after row of pigeon-holes, 'three handfulles in length, and ledged from hole to hole for them to walke upon'. An ingenious device called a potence allowed the keeper to reach any nest by means of a ladder which rotated on a central pillar passing within a couple of inches of the wall as it was pushed around. The interior was dim, to the liking of the pigeons, and each pair of birds had a double nest site

A typical Norman dovecot.

because before one set of squabs was ready to leave the nest the hen might well have laid her next clutch of eggs.

As time went by the pigeon houses improved in design and, especially in areas lacking local stone, they would be built of timber or brick and set on pillars. This had the great benefit of affording protection from predators such as rats, cats, weasels and squirrels. Hawks and owls were also a problem, and entrance holes, however carefully placed, attracted unwanted visitors. Heresbachius wrote in 1577: 'I found of late in myne own Dovehouse, an Owle sitting solemnly in the Nest upon her Egges in the middest of all the Pigions, by reason of the thickness of his feathers, yet will creep in at as little a place as the Pigion will; so small and little is their bodies, though they be bombased with feathers'.

Up on the roof, the pigeons would have a promenading area, sheltered from cold winds and facing south to catch the best of the sun. Under the whole structure there might well be room for a stable or cow house, giving the benefit of extra warmth in winter, to encourage breeding. Everything was done to aid these 'wondrous fruitfull' birds. Each year the best of the early squabs were carefully selected for breeding. The less satisfactory – 'unfruitefull and naughtie coloured, and otherwise faulty' – quickly found themselves being fattened for the table. But the right to husband pigeons was a privilege enjoyed by the chosen few – the nobility, the Lord of the Manor and the clergy – those who were powerful enough to be able to lay their hands on just a little spare corn in the winter. The peasants, and doubtless others as well, made do with clay pots set up to attract sparrows and starlings, from which they took the first broods of nestlings when they were fat enough to eat. This procedure, using wooden cistulae (flasks), was used in Silesia; and practised in Holland, with unglazed earthenware pots, in the late Middle Ages. In France they hung similar earthenware pots under the eaves of the houses in the region of Toulouse. When the Dutchmen came to drain the East Anglian fenlands in the mid-seventeenth century they brought the practice with them. Before this time sparrows had been paid as part of the rent, according to Norfolk rent books dating back to 1533, so one assumes the locals already had some knowledge of the technique.

For those whose status ran to it, pigeons offered a far better return than lowly sparrows. By the end of the seventeenth century, John Smyth could write of the Berkeley family of Gloucestershire: 'In each manor and almost upon each farm house he had a pigeon house, and in divers manors two. And in Hame and a few other (where his dwelling houses were) three: from

Pigeon holes on a farmhouse wall.

each house he drew yearly great numbers. As 1300, 1200, 1000, 850, 700, 650 from an house. And from Hame one year 2151 young pigeons.' These squabs must have represented an important source of revenue, fetching 2d a dozen, a worthwhile sum at that time.

Not only the fat squabs had value: the plentiful droppings which piled conveniently on the dovecot floor were rich in nitrogen and minerals. 'Doves dung is best of all others for Plants and Seeds, and may be scattered when anything is sown together with the seed, or at any time afterwards. One basketful therof is worth a cartload of sheep's dung. Our countrymen also are wont to sow Doves dung together with their grain' (Francis Willughby, *The Ornithology*, 1678). In Persia the dung was used to fertilise melon fields; in south-west France, where it was used in vineyards, dovecots were often kept as much for the value of the dung as the squabs.

Dung was also used in the tannery process, in removing hair from the hides, and as part of the process in making saltpetre for gunpowder. In addition it was used as a specific against the plague and the palsy. 'The flesh of young pigeons is restorative and useful to recruit the strength of such as are getting up or newly recovered from some great sickness' (Willughby, as above).

But the privileged aspects of pigeon-keeping involved social injustice. While they might be owned by the Lord of the Manor, the birds thought nothing of eating the peasant's or yeoman's corn. And lawyers offered no redress, as the jurist, John Selden, wrote in the early seventeenth century: 'Some men may make it a case of conscience whether a man may have a pigeon house, because his pigeons eat other folk's corn. But there is no such thing as conscience in the business: the matter is, whether he be a man of such quality that the state allows him to have a dove house; if so, there is an end of the business: his pigeons have a right to eat where they please themselves.' So the yeomen and tenant farmers gradually tore the shaky fabric of this law to pieces, building their own version of the free-standing pigeon houses, opening neat rows of nest-holes along the walls of their barns and farmhouses. But in any case the centuries of the pigeon house were coming to an end, and new agricultural practices made it possible to sustain more cattle and sheep through the winter months, this making butcher's meat available throughout the year. Most pigeon houses now lie derelict, while their inhabitants' descendants make a living in our city streets. Their truly wild ancestors have fared little better. Sadly, the wild coastal rock pigeon is becoming increasingly rare. A number of small populations of the

The pure-bred coastal rock doves are the root
stock of all dovecot and street pigeons.

pure-bred birds exist, confined to the north and west coasts, and Scottish and Irish islands. These are bluish-grey birds, with two striking black bars across the folded wing, and with neck and breast an iridescent purple and green. Apart from those far flung Celtic outposts of pure-bred birds, rock pigeons are now represented only by the cliffside colonies of racing pigeons which have given up the sport, and by the ubiquitous street pigeon which itself represents a hopeless mix of long-ago-escaped dovecot stock and more recent racing pigeon dropouts. Mixed or not, all domestic pigeons – racers, dovecot, messenger and fancy breeds – owe common ancestry to the rock pigeon, with its built-in suitability for intensive breeding in nestbox pigeon holes.

Wildfowl

Apart from pigeons, wildfowl have provided the earliest examples of artificial nesting devices. Various duck have been encouraged to nest in places convenient for their harvesting. Goldeneyes, for instance, nest naturally in tree holes or tree stumps, and by the late Middle Ages the Lapps were improving natural sites to attract them as a food source, mainly for the eggs.

Not long after the Viking colonisation of Iceland, coastal farmers realised the special qualities of the breast feathers of eiders. Lining the nest with its breast feathers, this sea duck arranges an eider-down quilt to cover and retain the warmth of the eggs if she leaves the nest for any reason. By the cunning provision of carefully placed sticks and stones (the birds like to nest *against* something), the farmers create conditions which suit the ducks and so encourage the formation of a colony in places which are convenient for the down collector. The practice is still followed today, and the farmers go to great lengths to please their worker birds, which are fortunately very tame. They provide music in the form of wind-activated instruments and hang coloured ribbons in string, both of which are supposed to act as added attractions. Some of the eider colonies are large, with anything up to 10,000 pairs nesting. The down is taken twice in each season, once just before the eggs hatch, when the lining is removed, and then later the remainder is taken after the young have left the nest. The down, which is carefully cleansed of any dirt and grass or large feathers, represents a substantial income to the farmers. They have a vested interest, of course, in making sure the wild duck breeds successfully and continues to patronise the facilities so carefully provided.

Eiders are one of the most numerous duck species in the world, their winter population in Europe totalling more than two million. Since the mid-

Eiders like to nest up against something, and
a fish box suits very well. Icelandic
farmers harvest their breast down feathers.

nineteenth century their range has been expanding and we now have
sizeable breeding numbers in Scotland – perhaps one day we shall see the
birth of a new British industry. In passing, we should note that the same
basic technique pioneered for attracting eiders to nest, that is the provision
of suitably shaped sticks or stones in a featureless landscape, has been used
by egg collectors wanting to plunder the eggs of greenshanks, whose
moorland nests are notoriously difficult to find. (Nowadays it is illegal to take
any eggs.)

Doubtless mallard ducks, and others, have been provided with convenient nest sites (convenient for the plunderer, that is) in Britain for
centuries, but it is not easy to find evidence of them. Decoys, which date
back to somewhere round the thirteenth century, were set to live-trap
migrant wildfowl in winter, and this practice certainly led to a small-scale
provision of nesting facilities in the breeding season. Perhaps the first record
of duck boxes in Britain comes from the diarist John Evelyn, a friend of
Samuel Pepys and a mine of information on the times of Charles II. In his
diary entry for 9 February 1665, he writes: 'I went to St James's Park . . . at
this time stored with numerous flocks of . . . wildfowl, breeding about the
Decoy, which for being so near so great a city, and among such a concourse
of soldiers and people, is a singular and diverting thing . . . There were withy-

In medieval times duck decoys provided fresh meat through the dark
days of winter, at a time when farmers could not maintain more
than their breeding stock. A 'judas' duck lured wild birds from the
open pond down the narrowing 'pipe' to their capture by the decoyman.

potts or nests for wildfowl to lay their eggs in, a little above the surface of the
water.' The designer of the decoy, incidentally, was a Dutchman who had
been brought over especially to do the job, Sydrach Hileus.

In North America, the Indians used nestboxes made from bottle gourds to
attract birds to nest and offer themselves as a food source. The disadvantage
of this method is that the gourd had to be smashed to get at the contents. But
they also, more effectively, farmed their wildfowl. Canada geese, relatively
tame and easy going in their choice of nest sites, were obvious targets. Over
the years they have been greatly exploited by men who found that they took
freely to haystacks and sheltered positions in the lee of a fence or hut.
Introduced to Britain as a status symbol to decorate the fashionable land-
scaped lake in the eighteenth century, they bred freely on the islands so

conveniently provided for them. Indeed, they flourished to become a common feral goose breeding all over England, a fair part of Wales and with outposts in Scotland. They enjoy popular protection in city parks and places like gravel pits and semi-natural reservoirs.

Black-headed gulls have been farmed for their eggs in times past. Breeding colonially, they patronise lake islands, sand and shingle banks at the coast and inland. From the eighteenth century onwards traditional gulleries were further encouraged by the preparation of man-made islands called hafts. In midwinter great quantities of reeds and rushes were cut and level places laid out to greet the return of the breeding birds in spring. These gulls lay in April, and the pairs were so numerous that at Scoulton Mere, East Dereham, in Norfolk, for instance, some 30,000 eggs were taken annually with 44,000 marking one particularly successful year. At Pallinsburn Hall, in Northumberland, a seven-acre lake was said to be 'covered so thick, when they are disturbed and on the wing, as if a shower of snow were falling on it'! (*History of British Birds*, F. O. Morris, 1857.) The young birds were also

Black-headed gulls nest sociably in a manner
that made them easy to exploit.

considered good eating, some gullery proprietors making fifty to eighty pounds a year by their sale. At the beginning of June, when the young were near fledging, they were driven onto the bank and netted, 'an occasion for jollity and Gentry'. In Staffordshire, three days of netting, over a period of a fortnight, gathered fifty dozen fat gull chicks at each drive.

Nestboxes for pleasure

So far, all these examples of artificial nestboxes or man-assisted nesting have had a culinary or commercial significance. Perhaps the first known record of birds attracted to an artificial nest site purely for aesthetic reasons, was that of Gilbert White's brother Thomas, who, as Gilbert recorded in his journal for 5 June 1782, 'nailed up several large scallop shells under the eaves of his house at South Lambeth, to see if the house martins would build in them. These conveniences had not been fixed half an hour before several pairs settled upon them; and expressing great complacency began to build immediately. The shells were nailed on horizontally with the hollow side upward; and should, I think, have a hole drilled in their bottoms to let off moisture from driving rains.'

The 'old gateway', Walton Hall.

Charles Waterton, whose pioneer wildlife reserve was described in chapter one, developed the use of nestboxes in the early nineteenth century, as also did the other pioneer field ornithologist, J. F. Dovaston. Unfortunately, although we know Dovaston used boxes in connection with his experiments, which may have been the first to consider the principles of territory in bird behaviour, he left precious little published information on them – a terrible lesson for all amateur scientists who fail to record their findings! Waterton wrote fully, so we know for example that he made (possibly in 1816) an artificial sand quarry with fifty deep holes in a sheltered and sunny part of the grounds of Walton Park. And we can imagine his pleasure and delight when, the very next summer, sand martins arrived in his reserve for the first time to found a thriving colony. (A similar experiment, equally successful, may be seen today at the RSPB's Minsmere reserve in Suffolk.)

Waterton improved hollow trees to make them more attractive for tawny owls, and developed a barn owl house 'on the ruin of the old gateway, against which, tradition says, the waves of the lake have dashed for the best part of a thousand years. I made a place with stone and mortar, about four feet square, and fixed a thick oaken stick firmly into it. In about a month or so

Waterton's owl-house and starling tower.

95

Back view of the gateway, showing the starling tower
and the ivy which Waterton encouraged.

after it was finished, a pair of barn owls came and took up their abode in it. I threatened to strangle the keeper if ever, after this, he molested either the old birds or their young ones.' Waterton was so delighted with his success that he subsequently built four other owl establishments, all of which were occupied. He also built a tower for jackdaws and starlings, rather in the style of a garden dovecot. Its stone pillar, smooth and vertical, was surmounted by a flat circular stone with sharply sloping edges, measures all designed to discourage rats. On top of this he placed a circular stone house, with conical roof, each course of stones having some loose ones, channelled to allow inspection access to the nest chamber behind. Although Waterton was regarded as little more than an eccentric in his own time, many of his ideas sowed the seeds of a whole new attitude to wildlife which were to bear a great deal of fruit later.

By 1897, twenty species were known to have bred in boxes or platforms of some kind in Britain. But the pioneer of large-scale bird manipulation by the use of nestboxes was the Baron von Berlepsch. His primary interest was the control of insect pests in his woodland, but there is no doubt he had aesthetic considerations firmly in mind. His main interest was in methods of increasing woodland bird populations in areas where foresters were intolerant of trees past their maturity, and nestboxes played an important part in his operations. Before his time, these devices had been relatively ineffective. He brought a cold and logical eye to the requirements and pursued them with relentless efficiency, pouring scorn on bird 'inventions' which had suffered failures in the past, not being based on what he saw as an understanding of bird nature.

Much of his experimentation, in the 500-acre bird park set aside for the purpose, lay in attempts to design the perfect woodpecker nestbox, having observed that woodpecker nest holes, deserted or uninhabited, were preferred nest sites by many other species. He proposed that his all-purpose box, whether destined for tits, nuthatches, starlings or indeed woodpeckers, was to resemble the natural woodpecker design in every exact respect. He proposed no mere invention, but exact copies of nature. He cut down several hundred trees in his search to reveal the woodpecker's secrets, discovering, to his surprise, that the nest cavities were all constructed to exactly the same general principles whether the carpenter was a black, green or spotted woodpecker. He then set about reproducing, in quantity, the perfect nestbox.

In fact, Berlepsch went too far, since as we know only too well, birds will occupy boxes of almost any shape, size or colour provided they offer certain fundamental design advantages – most particularly that the entrance hole is of the correct size. But, after measuring hundreds of natural woodpecker excavations, he specified that his boxes should reproduce those measurements precisely. He wouldn't allow tin guards around the entrance holes (to discourage great spotted woodpeckers from taking over from tits) on the grounds that they destroyed the natural appearance of the boxes ('their chief merit'), and said that such boxes were never inhabited, a claim which seems nonsensical today.

In one wood he set up 2000 of his boxes, and claimed ninety per cent occupancy; and in his bird park, he had 300 boxes occupied by birds of fourteen species. But although he went to some length to provide additional food for his birds in order to sustain an abundant population, it is not clear that he fully understood the overriding importance that food availability has in controlling bird numbers. He believed that the provision of nest sites was of paramount importance. Nevertheless, he was the first to make nestboxing popular; his boxes were successful, they were manufactured in large

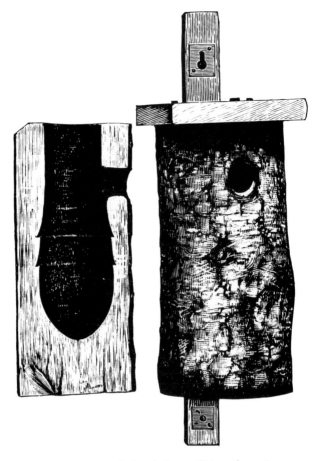

The Baron von Berlepsch designed his nestboxes to
reproduce a woodpecker's nest-hole exactly, believing
that this was the preference for most species.

quantities both in Germany and – under licence – abroad. In the early years
of this century the newly formed RSPB offered them in various sizes, for sale
at prices varying from 1s 6d (7½p) to 5s 6d (27½p). Berlepsch left his mark, if
nowhere else, on the commercial world of nestbox production, and it was
years before cheaper, less natural, but equally effective, versions were on
the market. In one major respect Berlepsch strayed off the path of righteous-
ness: he believed firmly in controlling predators, creatures he called the
enemies of his birds. These included cats, squirrels, weasels, martens,
polecats, house and tree sparrows, shrikes, sparrowhawks, goshawks, jays,

magpies and carrion crows – his blacklist for whose demise he offered rewards.

From Berlepsch's time, boxes were used systematically by scientists engaged in population studies. In the case of the pied flycatcher, which takes to nestboxes as ducks take to water, whole woodland populations have preferred the artificial sites to anything a tree has to offer, and tens of thousands of birds have been ringed in research directed towards analysing their life-style. A great deal of work has also been done on the nesting behaviour of blue and great tits, and of tawny owls.

Pied flycatchers take enthusiastically to nestboxes.

Improvement of natural nest sites

While bird table food is at best a poor substitute for natural food, man-assisted nest sites are very often a distinct improvement on the natural variety. Birds manage perfectly well without our help, of course, but the direct pruning of an awkward twig here and the enlargement of a hole there will often make a marginal nest site a prime one. A large, mature garden attached to a well-worn house will offer many desirable building sites to a house-hunting pair of birds. Standard trees and fruit trees provide strong foundations amongst their branches and, as they decay, cracks and openings allow access to secret cavities. Hedges and stone walls, old sheds and rickety eaves all allow birds to prospect and occupy likely spots. No possibility will be overlooked. Even a small garden and an over-maintained house will be colonised, especially if there is a nearby park, or some woodland, to improve food potential. From a bird's point of view, a newly constructed house with a raw garden is the least attractive prospect. For the bird gardener, he has all the enjoyment and anticipation of years of conscious construction and manipulation.

Crudely divided, there are birds which nest in holes and those which don't. Tits, nuthatches, starlings, tree sparrows and woodpeckers, for instance, live in secret caverns and crevices; robins, blackbirds and spotted flycatchers live out in the open, but for all that they are well concealed. Rooks and herons don't bother to conceal their nests, and instead site them comfortably high off the ground. Most seabirds, waders and waterfowl live out in the open for all to see, yet carefully choose places where they will be undisturbed for other reasons – high cliffs, remote places or islands.

Most woodland is managed for maximum timber production and decaying trees are not tolerated. So there is a chance for the bird gardener to redress the balance if he is able to allow an old and dying tree to live out its time undisturbed. It will give interest out of all proportion to its cash value. And if your tree is not decaying fast enough, encourage a nest site to develop by starting a hole or two with a suitable tool (eg a brace and bit) especially if there are some soft areas. Woodpeckers may take over and finish the job.

If you have no old trees in the garden it may make sense to import one. The famous film maker Eric Ashby spent a rewarding couple of seasons filming woodpeckers which had nested in a rotten birch. When they finally abandoned the tree he carefully sawed it down and took it home to set up again in a likely spot. If you do drill holes, or erect a tree-trunk, try to ensure a bit of shelter for the entrance and face it away from the hottest sun, which can exhaust nestlings.

Hedges offer a multitude of prime building sites for birds, especially when they are prickly enough to discourage predators. Hawthorn and holly are both excellent. Layered and trimmed, they provide dense cover for robins, dunnock, wrens, linnets, greenfinches and chaffinches, whitethroats and blackbirds, and so on. Beech and yew hedges also serve well, and although they are less prickly they are still difficult to penetrate. Very often you can improve their potential by judicious pruning of forked sites at about 5ft

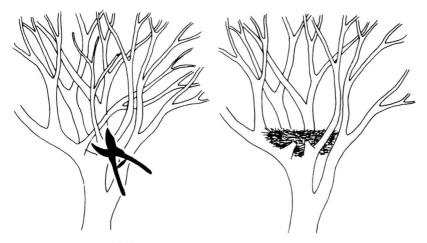

Judicious pruning makes it easier for birds
to build nests, but do it with care.

(1.5 m) level. Prune in autumn or winter to avoid disturbance at breeding time. Hazel needs special treatment, since it branches from the ground and lacks the forking structures which provide nest support. A little ingenuity is needed to devise some framework at a suitable height.

Cracks and crannies in sheds and stone walls are to be encouraged, providing near-natural homes for tits and wagtails. On an outside wall the ivy and honeysuckle you have grown for their food potential now give nesting possibilities in the breeding season for such as spotted flycatchers and blackbirds. Take out a brick or two from a wall and enlarge the hole behind it to make a welcome for a pied wagtail. For a grey wagtail, and a dipper, do the same thing in a bridge or culvert. Blackbirds will come indoors to an unfrequented shed and build on a shelf, as will swallows and robins. They all like to nest up *against* something – an old can or box perhaps. The cracks, crannies and wall ledges will be variously seen by different species as versions of their natural tree holes or sea cliff ledges. So enlarge holes to $1\frac{1}{8}$ in (29 mm) for tits, and ensure there are larger entrance holes, always open, so that swallows and other birds can find their way into the garage or potting shed.

There are endless possibilities for creating natural or near-natural nest sites and it is really more a question of improvisation than anything else, based on a study of the bird's natural requirements. Obviously it is import-ant to avoid a situation in which a bird's home may be too easily discovered. And don't improve a site which has already proved successful.

101

Spotted flycatchers like to nest against a creeper-clad wall.

Nestboxes, artificial nests, rafts and ledges

The object of providing nestboxes is that it increases the number of potential building sites for prospecting birds, and that it makes fairly close observation of their life-style possible. The facilities offered by the box must conform, in essentials, to those which are sought by the particular species for which it is designed. These will fall somewhere into the two basic categories: an enclosed box with entrance hole; and an open tray or ledge, with or without sides and roof. The closed type tends to be the most successful, partly because the average house and garden doesn't offer many convenient cavities reached by a suitable tunnel, and mainly because most of the birds which are prepared to live close to us derive from a woodland habitat.

Nestboxes are readily available from commercial suppliers (see the advertisements in the RSPB's magazine *Birds*, and the birdwatchers' monthly magazine, *British Birds*). But beware of novelty designs which owe more to sentiment than biological requirement, ie boxes whose dimensions are incorrectly formulated or which offer footholds to predators in the shape of ornamental windows and chimneys and, in some cases, unnecessary perches. Rustic boxes, made of hollowed-out birch branches, are perfectly satisfactory, although the wood deteriorates rapidly and they don't last many seasons. But there seems little point in going to all the trouble of making them when they are usually fixed to almost any tree but a birch, thus losing the possible advantage of camouflage. Plain square boxes are the easiest to make, and there is precious little evidence that the birds mind one way or another. The interior size, entrance hole size and the placing of the box are what counts most.

Since tit boxes are most people's introduction to the nestboxing craft it might be most useful to consider their construction in some detail. Other boxes, suitable for other species with different requirements, can then be dealt with in terms of habitats. The drawing below shows how to mark up a piece of boarding, 41 in × 6 in (104 cm × 15 cm), to cut out the pieces for one standard box. The ¾ in (18 mm) timber is thick enough to afford good insulation and to last a reasonable length of time. Softwood such as old floorboarding is usually the right size and is well seasoned and ideal. Cedar

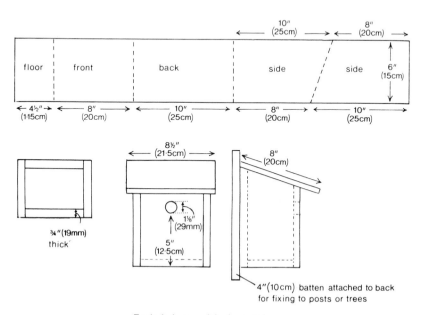

Exploded view of the basic tit box.

weathers well and needs little maintenance. Hardwood will prove more weather resistant – oak is best – but is more difficult to work with and is prone to splitting, quite apart from being expensive (unless you can get offcuts from a mill). Seasoned material has the great advantage over green or fresh-cut wood in that the latter is likely to warp and split as it dries. The interior surface need not be planed, as a roughened one offers a grip to the chicks as they come to scramble out of the nest.

The insulation properties of the material are worth consideration. It has been shown that a warmer nestbox encourages earlier laying by great tits, for instance, and thereby increases the chances of success for the clutch. The laying date of the hen is influenced by her ability to feed sufficiently well to make an egg every day, as well as nourish herself. So, if the bird roosts in a relatively warm nestbox before the breeding period, she is in laying condition at the earliest possible time.

Plastic materials suffer from the bugbear of internal condensation and the danger of chick loss from damp conditions. Concrete has the disadvantage of being heavy and difficult to fix in place. A felt roof may be stripped by squirrels, a thatched roof may be plundered by sparrows. On the whole, timber is probably the most convenient nestbox material.

The interior size is critical. In the case of great and blue tits the floor area should be at least 4 in × 4 in (100 mm × 100 mm). In our plan we have allowed for a more generous 6 in × 4½ in (15 cm × 11.5 cm). If the floor is larger than this it merely forces the tits into importing unnecessarily large quantities of material to form foundations for the nest cup. You may feel the dimensions of the interior of the box are surprisingly small, but the incubating birds adopt a squatting position which uses little space, and there is no need to accommodate their stretched length. Also, when the chicks are hatched they will benefit from the warmth of a jumble of bodies, provided there is enough room for them to stretch their wings.

Allow the sides to extend a short distance below the floor, so that draining water rots the wall bottoms before it begins to rot the floor section. The roof or an upper wall section should be removable, so that you can inspect the contents and carry out routine maintenance. The standard RSPB tit box (see opposite) has a front section which lifts out, and the advantage of this choice is that there is less likely to be trouble with a leaking roof, but it does need to fit snugly and securely when in position. There is probably no need for a lifting roof except when it is necessary to trap the parents for ringing, weighing and general inspection (when the entrance hole will need to be plugged). If this method is chosen, then the roof may be attached to a suitably upward extended back wall with a piece of rubber inner tube or leather. Another advantage of the RSPB box is that by removing the entrance-hole section the box is converted to a semi-open plan layout suitable for robins, spotted flycatchers and pied wagtails.

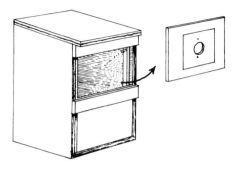

Dual-purpose nestbox. Remove panel for open-plan nesters. Note the metal guard-plate which discourages attack by woodpeckers when the box is used for tits.

For hole nesters like tits, though, the entrance must definitely not be at floor level. The birds need to import a quantity of nest material which will occupy a few inches at the bottom of the box, and in any case the chicks would be extra vulnerable to predators if there was an opening at their nest cup level. There is no need for a back door or tradesman's entrance to the box. The single entrance hole must be near the top, on any side, at least 5 in (12.5 cm) from the floor, thus containing the nestlings and discouraging cats' paws which might fish them out. Tits prefer a very small entrance hole, another feature which makes theft difficult for cats. A $1\frac{1}{8}$ in (29 mm) diameter hole will allow easy access for both blue and great tits. Blue tits are just able to manage a 1 in (25 mm) entrance, but the tolerance takes some achieving if you really want to exclude the dominant great tit in favour of the smaller bird. A $1\frac{1}{4}$ in (32 mm) hole fairly precisely defeats house sparrows, but not tree sparrows, which can be equally persistent in their efforts. They may, on occasion, fill a box which has frustrated their entry with nest material, thus effectively spoiling it for the use of other birds. As the indefatigable Baron von Berlepsch said, 'where success with nesting boxes is aimed at, the fight against sparrows must not be overlooked.' A $1\frac{1}{2}$ in (38 mm) hole excludes starlings, which are unable to squeeze through.

Once you have achieved your desired blue tits, don't be tempted to increase the size of the hole when you see them pecking at the entrance.

They are not trying to make it larger in order to get in more easily – tits just tend to peck at anything. If the holes are too large, incidentally, nuthatches will plaster them with mud to reduce them to a size which suits.

Do not include any kind of perch, intended to allow the incoming or outgoing bird a place to rest and fold its wings, before it negotiates the hole. Study of movie film has shown that they close their wings with great facility in order to pass through, and the exterior of the box is a dangerous place where they have no desire to loll about. Perches only serve to make life easier for cats and weasels. There is need for a clear, uncluttered flight path to the hole, giving room for the spread of full wingspan right up to the entrance.

Perch sticks make theft easier for weasels.

Nestbox construction does not need to be to a high standard of carpentry. The completed work must be windproof and rainproof, and if this is achieved by liberal use of sealants the birds will not complain. A poor fit around floor level has the advantage of providing vital water drainage.

Inevitably water of some kind finds its way into the box, and the down feathers of nestlings are no protection. The chicks are susceptible to chilling and subsequent exhaustion. Be careful to achieve a rainproof roof, and make sure drips do not find their way through the entrance hole. Bore ventilation holes in the floor section, and also one or two in the top of the wall where it gets some protection from the roof. But don't make the holes big enough to encourage a queen bumble bee or tree wasps to enter and prospect the interior as a possible hive. This means the holes must be less than ³⁄₁₆ in (4 mm) in diameter unless they are covered by gauze. Queen bees do have a tendency to overwinter in nestboxes, and then proceed to found a colony. But the chance is not great, and it has to be said that the bees ought to be welcome.

Use copper or galvanised nails, or brass screws, to assemble your nestboxes. Ordinary nails will soon rust and the box disintegrate. A coat of preservative (cuprinol or creosote) will protect softwood boxes. There seems little point in going to the trouble of painting the box, just to make it more easily seen by predators or small boys! However, natural wood colours, or browns or greens, are acceptable. Interestingly, a ten-year colour trial was carried out by *Audubon*, a magazine published in the United States, which found that red was the most attractive colour for boxes, closely followed by green, then blue, with yellow well down the occupancy list. For some curious reason the test did not include natural wood boxes, or black or white ones, so I don't think we can learn much from it. On the whole it seems likely that the external appearance of the box is not very important to the bird – its concern is with the indoor facilities.

Siting the box is a critical affair. The main criteria are protection from the elements and from enemies. First consider the life-style of the intended occupant when you choose a place for it. Tit boxes should be attached to walls or trees, or anything which makes some kind of substitute for a tree, which is where they will be looking for likely entrance holes. The open plan boxes for blackbirds, robins and spotted flycatchers should be placed against a wall where they are hidden in a dense jungle of ivy or some other creeper, or in a thick hedge, or in a fruit tree where there is some cover, and so on. They are best fixed in discreet crutch sites, invisible to the outside world. The birds will find them.

It has been said that the best time to erect a nestbox is in October or November, so that it has time to blend in with its surroundings and give potential occupiers plenty of time to discover and consider its possibilities, and also because birds (and various mammals and insects, for that matter) might roost in it during winter. But it seems to me that the box should be erected as soon as it is available. The roosting and evaluating phase is doubtless useful, but there are plenty of records of songbirds, and kestrels, too, taking over a nest box on more or less the day it was erected.

Most garden nest boxes should be fixed at about 5 ft to 6 ft (1.5 m to 1.8 m) above the ground. Factors such as possible disturbance will obviously affect the decision, and it is worth remembering that birds will nest at heights ranging from ground level to tree top. In order to protect them from hot sun and wet Atlantic winds, the general rule is that the opening should face somewhere in the arc from north through east to south-east, but if it is well sheltered this question of orientation is probably not significant. Nestboxes do not need to be hidden away in a dense clump of trees, or in the middle of a vast woodland. It is better to site them at the edge of a copse, or ride, at the interface between lawn or grass field and the trees. This is the kind of country which gives the best feeding return. There must be an uninterrupted flight path to the entrance, and a distinct lack of places for cats to lie in wait. A convenient staging post some 6 ft (1.8 m) away may be an asset. This can be anything from a clothes-line to a twig, by way of a specially stuck-in post.

Firm fixing for nestboxes is not a prime requirement; after all, birds often build nests in places which sway with the wind. Even boxes which literally hang from tree branches are successful. But for all that it probably makes good sense to fix securely, and no one, least of all the occupant, wants the box to collapse because of an inadequate screw or rusty nail. And fix the box by way of a batten which will help to ensure that it does not become

Try to fix a box so that it avoids the worst of the rain.

permanently wet and disintegrates prematurely. Many clutches are drowned in natural nest-sites every year, so take particular care to see that rainwater cannot find its way into the box, remembering that a lot of rain trickles down a wall or tree trunk, and that it tends to follow well-established channels. Make sure the box stands proud of them, or to one side. Incline the box outwards with a slight slant, so that drips from the projecting roof do not go through the entrance hole. Do not worry if the floor of the box, when set up, it is not quite horizontal. The birds will solve this problem when they import nest material.

If you want to erect the box against a particularly fine tree which it would be sad to damage, use trenails as the old-time shipwrights did when nailing planks to frames in 'wooden walls'. These conical pegs of oak or iroko will do the job perfectly well and will not damage the tree (or the saw in due course). Alternative choices are to use plastic-covered wire and 'whip' the box to the branch (but this will have to be replaced each season to avoid constricting growth), or to use copper nails which are relatively soft and kind to the forester's saw. Otherwise use 3 in galvanised nails like most of us and grit your teeth.

It is not easy to suggest the number of boxes you should erect for any given species. The quantity depends both on the availability of natural sites and on the local food potential, natural and artificial. But first consider the life-style of your intended occupant. It is a waste of time, for example, to

Robins are exceptionally aggressive in defence of their property.

expect two pairs of robins to set up house in close proximity. Though it may well make sense to put up more than one box in the hope of getting one occupied. Robins are fiercely territorial, blackbirds slightly less so, but they won't object to other species living close by. So your robin boxes can be close to tit boxes. Tits, too, are aggressive, status-seeking birds, so don't put tit boxes too close to one another. Three or four boxes to the acre is probably a useful rule of thumb.

Some birds, which are highly sociable at other times, go solo when they contemplate breeding. Starlings are a good example, preferring to establish family independence at breeding time. Others remain colonial, enjoying sociability and the safety of numbers. House martins, once they have taken to a site, will tend to flock to it and there may be dozens of mud huts around the eaves of a favourable house. Swifts and sparrows, too, subscribe to the jolly principle of the more the merrier.

Songbird nestboxes may be primed with a layer of moss or a plaited ring of straw, to make them even more attractive to house-hunters, but this is unlikely to be an important consideration in determining whether the box will be 'bought' or not. But willow tits will only ever use a box which has been jammed solid with woodshavings or polystyrene chips, so that they can excavate the cavity themselves. Woodpeckers may just possibly be impressed with the sight of a few wood chippings at the bottom of their box.

As with the robins, and indeed many other species, the male blue tit has the job of finding likely sites and he then takes the female to see them. She chooses, then cleans it in preparation for nest building. The cleaning may not be very thorough, and frequently they will simply build on top of an old nest. The corners will be filled and a foundation of mosses and grasses laid. And it is at this point we can enjoy the pleasure of providing nest material from a 'builder's yard', although we must under no circumstances try to join in with the job of building. Not surprisingly, birds tend to make use of the building materials which are most conveniently at hand. Nests in trees tend to be made of twigs, those on cliffs of seaweed and driftwood, on beaches of pebbles, on moorland – heather. And in a factory – bits of wire!

If you provide suitable materials, birds will enthusiastically collect them. In the breeding season, when the scrap and peanut cages are not required for food, they can be packed with straw, feathers, dog or cat combings, *short* bits of cotton, cotton-wool, sheep wool, etc. In the garden, this may reduce the amount of thieving the sparrows and jackdaws will indulge in when they try to unravel the string from your beanpoles, or tease out threads from your clothes on the washing-line. Tree species will prefer your offerings to be hung from the branches. But put some at ground level, in a mesh bag perhaps, firmly pegged so that they can't be carried away in bulk.

If the weather is particularly dry in May, when the house martins are busy plastering their nestcups, it may be helpful to pour a couple of buckets of water over the earth in a likely place, eg along a dusty country lane or over a well-worn bare earth patch on the lawn or in a park. They sometimes have difficulty in finding mud puddles for which to pick up their nest gobbets.

The collection of nest material offers an opportunity to the newly engaged pair of birds to reinforce their pair bond, when they offer and exchange particularly choice pieces. In the case of rooks, for instance, you will see them, at the chosen nest site, excitedly passing sticks to and fro with much exaggerated posturing and ritual exchanges of compliments. And, for many species, when the nest is completed the exchanges will continue, the cock bird offering choice food morsels instead of twigs in the ritual courtship feeding – a procedure which provides the female with nourishment to help form the eggs and keep her alive during the period of incubation. The hens of some species obtain more than a third of their food from their mates during the early part of the feeding season.

Swifts find some of their nest material
in flight, collecting down and feathers.

Whatever the type of nest, and wherever it is built, whether in nestbox or natural site, its object is the same – to create a cup which will hold the eggs in warmth and yet retain a measure of security from predators and shelter from the elements. It may range from the casual few twigs of a pigeon to the most elaborate nursery of a goldfinch. (In the case of some seabirds and raptors, there may be no nest at all, but in those cases the eggs are well protected by other factors.)

Do not disturb the sitting bird in your
nestbox, in case you betray it to a predator.

If you *are* lucky enough to be successful in enticing a breeding pair to your nestbox, keep any inspection to a minimum. Be thoughtful with your photography, and in particular be extremely sensitive with any 'gardening' you may be tempted to do with natural nests which don't quite suit your angle of view. You may, inadvertently, betray the nest to a predator. If you are recording the career of your nests for the British Trust for Ornithology's Nest Record Scheme (see page 171), keep your visits to a minimum. The well-being and safety of the birds is paramount – put their interests first. If you want to count the young, wait a few days from hatching in the case of small birds. And don't creep up on the nest with exaggerated fairy footfalls. Better to let them know you're coming. It is also important not to disturb nests at the stage when their occupants are close to leaving, since there is a danger they might 'explode' away and become exposed too soon to the attention of the world at large. However, if this disaster should occur, collect up the chicks in a handkerchief as best you may and post them back home. Then block up the entrance for ten minutes or so, until they have quietened down.

Every year the newspapers enjoy a silly bird season where nests are photographed in every conceivable odd position. Blackbirds and pied wagtails have nested in every known make of motor vehicle, including aircraft, and often fledged their young successfully in spite of daily trips to the office and back! Rooks have colonised the vertical ladders on the side of refinery chimneys, seeing them as perfect substitutes for trees in an increasingly treeless landscape. And black guillemots nested on the Yell Ferry in the Shetlands, providing the young with daily trips long before they were scheduled to go to sea!

Unhatched eggs, dead or disappearing juveniles, are a distressing possibility. Any number of causes may account for them, apart from the natural loss to predators. A dead parent, inexperienced first-time parents who may have failed in their duty, shortage of food at a critical time – all are possibilities. Double check to see whether rainwater, or cold winds, or the sun's heat, or a cat perch, were responsible. And if you are reasonably certain the fault was not yours, reflect that a natural event of this kind is the normal end for an enormous number of nestlings. It is something which is part of the expected scheme of things, not to be dwelled upon unduly.

Many clutches of eggs and broods of young chicks will be lost to squirrels, weasels, cats, crows, and great spotted woodpeckers. The loss rate is highest in the case of open nests, particularly when it is early on in the season and they are least concealed by growing leaves. But even the most sturdily built nestbox will be the subject of attack from the ground and the air. Cats will try to hook the contents out with their paws, or lie in wait, sitting on top of the box. Weasels are common garden predators – they are good climbers and able to squirm through even a $1\frac{1}{8}$ in (29 mm) blue tit hole to fish out the eggs or chicks. Grey squirrels simply reach in for their reward, and if the roof or lid or removable wall-piece is not secure, they will knock it off. They may even gnaw their way in by enlarging the entrance. The only remedy for this is to plump for a concrete nestbox (with the disadvantages of weight and tendancy to overheat), or to protect the entrance hole with one of the metal plates which the RSPB will supply (see page 181 for address). Tying a bundle of gorse branches around the tree trunk, or even around the box itself, will be a deterrent, especially to cats. However, this remedy will not affect the nest raiding propensities of the great spotted woodpecker, a persistent robber. They too will dislodge a loose lid, or enlarge the entrance by

Like other crows, magpies are skilled egg thieves,
and they are becoming much commoner in suburban
gardens where they are not persecuted.

chipping until it is big enough for them to get in. The metal RSPB plate may do the trick, but with woodpeckers there is the problem that they simply drill themselves a side entrance with their chisel bills to effect an entry. If they are really troublesome then a concrete box is the answer. Given the chance, these woodpeckers will take young house martins and sparrows, as well as tits.

One other hazard which nestbox users face is that sparrows and starlings may take them over from their rightful owners, or intended owners, by sheer brute force. But this is all part of the rich warp and woof of bird life.

At the end of the breeding season, in say September and October (but remember that some species, even tits very occasionally, raise more than one brood), remove the used nests and give the boxes an anti-bug spray. The nests and box crevices will be home for feather lice, mites, ticks and flea larvae – creatures which can survive long periods without their host – so you will need to dust with Malathion or some other safe insecticide. A squirt of pyrethrum dust would do the job, or perhaps an end-of-season coat of creosote or Cuprinol. Then it will be ready for a winter let. Moths may over-winter in them, perhaps even toads, mice or bats. Great and blue tits will certainly use them for winter warmth, roosting in solitary splendour. They often take to rather over-lit, but centrally heated, street lamps for overnight roosts. House martins, which frequently produce three broods of young and whose breeding season will often extend into November, roost in family parties in their nest cavities, which must make for a tight fit.

Wrens are the record holders for mass nestbox occupation. Although they are reluctant to nest in the boxes, they use them enthusiastically for the

Wrens rarely breed in nestboxes, but they use them
as roost-places, sometimes in astonishing numbers.

winter warmth they provide. Severe winters hit them hard. Their preferred food is insects and they must work hard to get enough fuel to survive the cold nights. As small birds, with a lot of surface area relating to their volume, they suffer a great deal from heat loss and have a pressing need for warmth. At night they tend to huddle together in old nests or holes, and nestboxes suit perfectly, with the added advantage of good thermal insulation.

Thirty or forty wrens commonly creep into their chosen roost box, and the record to date is an astonishing sixty-one, which patronised a box $4\frac{1}{2} \times 5\frac{1}{2} \times 5\frac{3}{4}$ in (11.5 cm $\times$ 14 cm $\times$ 14.6 cm) large in Norfolk. Apparently, the last arrivals were so desperate to get into the warmth that they grouped themselves together and barged in the entrance hole as a scrum – there's strength in numbers. In that astonishing case, only one of the birds was found dead in the morning, but this was presumably the effect of cramped quarters on a bird which was already in poor condition. It seems unlikely to be suffocation which causes mortality in these circumstances. The bird's metabolism slows down at night, with reduced requirement for oxygen. So even if you have a party of would-be record breakers using your tit box, don't bore any holes to increase ventilation – the wrens are coming in because of the warmth, not the fresh air.

Give the boxes a spring clean before the breeding season, cleaning out any droppings left by the winter occupants, and another squirt of pyrethrum will kill the bugs.

Systematic list of birds which patronise nestboxes and artificially-provided nest sites

This list is assembled in the internationally accepted Voous order of classification, its advantage lying in the fact that the birds are arranged in a sequence of related families which makes taxonomic sense. An alphabetical list is provided in the general index at the back of this book.

The notes refer first to status and distribution, then to the natural nest-site and nest of the bird, then to the artificially provided device, and finishes with basic clutch data.

NB 'Interior depth' refers to the distance from the bottom of the entrance hole to the floor of the box, *not* from floor to ceiling.

Diver, red-throated   *Gavia stellata*
Local in Scottish Highlands, islands, Orkney, Shetland and Donegal.

Nests close to water, within 1 yd (1 m) or so, usually on islets, sometimes at lochside. A mere scrape in the vegetation; sometimes a platform of vegetation.

Artificial nest site: In Argyll, where the divers were suffering from a good deal of disturbance both by fishermen and hydro-electric scheme water fluctuations, local enthusiasts found that the birds would accept a raft as a nest-site. Empty plastic containers topped with heavy gauge wire netting, planted with turves and bound with yet more wire netting, were anchored in suitable hill lochs.

Eggs: Usually 2 yellowish-olive to brown. Late May or June. Incubation 24–29 days, fledging about 8 weeks. One brood.

Diver, black-throated *Gavia arctica*
Local in Scottish Highlands. Large lochs.

See Diver, red-throated.

Grebe, great crested *Podiceps cristatus*
Breeds regularly in most English counties except the far south-west. Scarcer in Scotland and Wales. Lakes, reservoirs, gravel pits and large ponds with ready cover.

Nests naturally among reeds or vegetation close to water's edge. Water plants, reeds, perhaps twigs, just above surface.

Artificial nest site: May adopt the sort of raft put up by wildfowl enthusiasts for geese and ducks (see page 119).

Eggs: Usually 3–4 chalky white, become grained duration incubation. End March onwards. Incubation 28 days; fledging 9–10 weeks. Sometimes two broods.

Fulmar *Fulmarus glacialis*
Summer visitor, breeding on coastal cliffs more or less round the whole of the British Isles.

Nests on cliff slopes and ledges, on bare rock or soil. Sometimes the female makes a slight hollow.

Artificial nest site: Has taken to excavated ledges provided in Norfolk cliffs, along stretches where there are few natural sites. On exposed cliffs, where there are patches of sand in the boulder clay, dig out a ledge about 1 ft (30 cm) wide and 6 in to 8 in (15 cm to 20 cm) deep in the sand. The birds do the rest.

Eggs: White. Late May. Incubation 8 weeks; fledging 8 weeks. One brood.

Heron, grey *Ardea cinerea*

Resident throughout British Isles, wherever there is water not too deep to wade in.

Nests in tree canopies, colonially. Single nests sometimes found which may signal the founding of a new colony. Bulky structure of branches, sticks, lined with smaller twigs.

Artificial nest site: May take advantage of a platform on chicken wire frame firmly placed high in Scots pine or other suitable tree.

Eggs: 3–5 greenish-blue. February or March. Incubation about 25 days; fledging about 50–55 days. Sometimes two broods.

Swan, mute *Cygnus olor*

Generally distributed. Open water, ponds, parks, sheltered estuaries, sea coast and lochs.

Nests almost anywhere near water, on large heap of vegetation.

Artificial nest site: Takes readily to a suitable raft, both on freshwater and on estuaries.

Eggs: 5–7 almost white, tinged with greyish- or bluish-green. April or May. Incubation about 35 days; fledging about $4\frac{1}{2}$ months. One brood. *Warning*: aggressive at nest.

Goose, greylag *Anser anser*

In summer, hilly heather moors, islands. Feral birds breed more freely by freshwater sites such as reservoirs, gravel pits and lakes, mainly in islands.

Nests on the ground. Heather or twigs, grasses, mosses, with down and feathers.

Artificial nest site: Has regularly nested on rafts in suitable locations.

Eggs: 4–6 creamy white. Last half of April. Incubation 27–28 days; fledging about 8 weeks. One brood.

Goose, Canada *Branta canadensis*

Was introduced to Britain as a status symbol, ornamenting stately lakes, in eighteenth century. Has since become a successful feral species, enjoying grassland and marshes by freshwater ponds and lakes.

Nests on islands and marshes, sheltered by undergrowth or bush. Hollow-lined with grasses, leaves, reeds, down and feathers.

Artificial nest site: Box or platform raised on posts above water level or on raft. Make an artificial island, plant clumps of iris, reeds, sedge, etc to provide a nest site. Since the expansion of gravel pit workings of the last few decades

Canada goose at the nest.

they have taken advantage of the spoil islands which remain when the pits are worked out and flooded.

In Canada, where they sometimes nest in suitable tree sites such as broken stumps or in the hollows left by fallen branches, this propensity has been exploited by egg thieves. Wooden platforms, up to 65 ft (20 m) above ground, or on top of 10 ft (3 m) poles where there are no trees, are soon colonised. Try sawn-off barrels or open tubs, suitably drained, and offering a platform some 2 ft (60 cm) across and 1 ft (30 cm) deep. *Warning:* Canada geese, especially the gander, can be aggressive in the breeding season.

Eggs: 5 or 6 white. Late March or April. Incubation 4 weeks; fledging 6 weeks. One brood.

Shelduck *Tadorna tadorna*

Generally distributed round low-lying coast and estuaries.

Nests in rabbit burrows, bramble tunnels, in gorse and bracken, sometimes in walls, hollow trees. Down with some vegetation.

119

9"(23cm) diameter
drainpipe

12"(30cm) cube
timber nest chamber

A shelduck nest-tunnel.

Nestbox: May be persuaded to nest in a fruit box in a hollow in vegetation, for instance wild rose or bramble bushes surrounded by long grass or bracken. Or sink a small barrel into the ground, with just a 6 in (15 cm) entrance hole showing. Provide a 1 ft (30 cm) cube nest chamber approached by a length of 9 in (23 cm) drain pipe. Simulate a rabbit burrow. (May also be successful for Manx shearwaters, storm petrels and puffins, in suitable habitat.)

Eggs: 8–15 creamy-white. May. Incubation, 28 days; fledging 45 days. One brood.

Gadwall   *Anas strepera*
Breeding bird in Britain since mid-nineteenth century, having been introduced to East Anglia. Scattered over British Isles, breeds by shallow, lowland sheets of freshwater, lakes, meres, reservoirs, marshes and slow-flowing streams. Spreading slowly.

Nest site is concealed in dense vegetation close to water, tussocky grass, sedge, nettles.

Artificial nest site: May nest on rafts, if provided with good growth of vegetation.

Eggs: 8–12 creamy-buff. May or early June. Incubation 27–28 days; fledging 7 weeks. One brood.

Mallard   *Anas platyrhynchos*
Generally distributed, near all kinds of freshwater, estuaries and coastal islands.

Nests in thick undergrowth sometimes far from water. Pollard willows, tree holes, second-hand crow nests, etc. Grass, leaves, rushes, feathers, down.

Mallards on village pond.

Nestbox: Try providing an apple-box or large, open cat basket in typical nesting area. Where mallards have become very tame (village ponds and the like), try erecting an open-ended barrel on an island. Otherwise a mere hollow in the ground, bordered by a couple of short logs and sheltering under a wigwam of spruce boughs, may do the trick. Mallard nests are probably best sited on rafts or islands, where they enjoy some protection from foxes and rats.

Alternative nestbox: Using sawmill offcuts, make a box with inside dimensions of 1 ft (30 cm) square and 9 in (23 cm) high. Prime with an inch or two (25 to 50 mm) of woodshavings. Make a funnel about a foot (30 cm) long leading to an entrance hole 6 in (15 cm) square. This tunnel entrance serves to deter crows. A ramp should lead gently down from the tunnel entrance to the ground. This ease of access is important, not only for the comfort of the duck, but because she might take broods back to the safety of the box at night for the first couple of weeks after leaving the nest, especially in cold weather. NB: A duck-box may well be taken over by moorhens.

Eggs: About 12 greyish-green or greenish-buff, occasionally a clear pale blue. February onwards. Incubation 4 weeks; fledging 7½ weeks. One or two broods.

Goldeneye *Bucephala clangula*

A few pairs now established in Scotland and increasing with many of those present using nestboxes.

In Scandinavia, goldeneyes nest in tree holes and stumps, beside lakes and ponds in thickly wooded country. In late Middle Ages they were farmed for eggs by Lapps who improved natural nesting-sites.

Nestbox: Like most hole-nesters, from blue tits to tawny owls, goldeneyes take readily to artificial nests. They returned to breed in Scotland in 1971, using boxes which had been first erected twenty years before. Scottish highland lochs offer ideal habitat, but nest sites are scarce in the wild, so boxes seem the ideal answer. Make as for mallards, but fix them up to 33 ft (10 m) above ground, arranging the entrance tunnel so that there is a porch and a 90° turn before they reach the nest chamber. Like tits, they fly straight in, and do not need a landing perch. NB If you do get them you will need NCC approval to inspect the box.

Eggs: 6–15 bluish-green. Mid April on. Incubation 26–30 days; fledging 57–60 days. One brood.

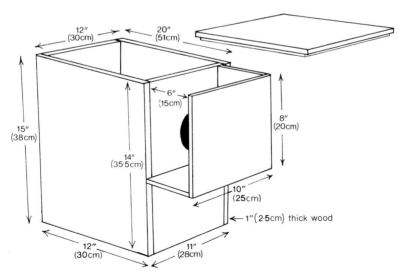

Goldeneye nestbox with lid removed.

Duck, tufted *Aythya fuligula*

Local but fairly widely distributed, except in the south-west. Lakes, lochs and reservoirs.

Nests close to water in tussocks of sedge or rushes.

Artificial nest-site: May occasionally nest on rafts.

Eggs 6–14 greenish-grey. Second half of May, June. Incubation 23–26 days; fledging 6–7 weeks. One brood.

Kestrel *Falco tinnunculus*

Resident, generally distributed, except in winter in far north. Moors, coast, farmland and open woodland, suburbs and cities.

Makes no nest, but uses a scrape on cliff or quarry ledge or uses second-hand crow nest as platform. Sometimes in tree hollow or ledge on building or ruin.

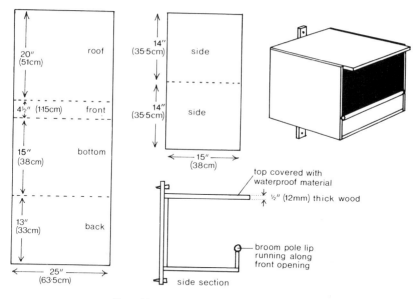

Kestrel boxes have been highly successful.

Nestbox: Open-fronted, 25 in × 15 in × 15 in (63.5 cm × 38 cm × 38 cm) high, with roof overhanging a couple of inches (5 cm). One of the long sides is partly open, having only a 5 in (12.5 cm) board along the bottom part, fitted with a broom pole lip to enable the bird to perch easily before entering. Prime the box with some peat mould or woodshavings. Fix very firmly on 18 ft to 30 ft (6 m to 10 m approx) pole, or high on side of house where some shelter is available from midday sun. If fixed to tree, make sure chick thieves cannot climb to it easily (there is a ready illegal market for juvenile kestrels). And place it so that wing-exercising juveniles can step out onto a branch.

In Holland, where farmers erect these boxes to encourage kestrels in controlling voles and shrews, they have been highly successful.

Eggs: About 5, the white colour often hidden by red-brown splotchings. Mid April onwards. Incubation 28 days; fledging 28 days. One brood.

Moorhen *Gallinula chloropus*

Generally distributed, scarcer in northern Scotland. Almost any freshwater from a ditch to a lake.

Nests typically in shallow, still water. Platform of dead plants amongst aquatic vegetation, in trees and bushes.

Nestbox: Will happily take over a duck box.

Eggs: 5–11 whitish-grey to buff or greenish eggs. April onwards. Incubation 19–22 days; fledging 6–7 weeks. Usually two broods, frequently three.

Coot *Fulica atra*

Generally distributed, except in highlands. Lakes, large ponds, slow-flowing rivers and backwaters.

Nest is large platform of vegetation built up well above water level, among reeds or in open.

Artificial nest site: Has regularly nested on rafts.

Eggs: 6–9 stone-coloured, spotted dark brown. Second week March onwards. Incubation 21–24 days; fledging about 8 weeks. One, sometimes two, occasionally three broods.

Tern, common *Sterna hirundo*

Breeds colonially round most of British coast and inland in Scotland and Western Ireland.

Nests in low-lying sandbanks or shingle beaches, low rocky islets and skerries. Inland on islets in lochs and low moorland, river shingle banks.

Artificial nest site: Has nested on rafts. The Merseyside Ringing Group moored a raft on a reservoir belonging to the British Steel Corporation. Based on a frame of telegraph poles it was decked with railway sleepers and covered with slag, shingle and grass sods. Blocks of expanded polystyrene gave buoyancy. The finished raft – 100 sq ft (30 sq m) of tern surface – buoyant enough to carry three men, was secured by nylon lines to scrap iron anchors. While the surroundings might have been incongruous, the raft was effective in providing a nesting place and an old-established ternery was able to maintain its presence, thus reversing a trend towards decline. To be worth all this effort, though, the raft must be close to a food source for the terns.

Eggs: Usually 3 stone-coloured. Late May or early June, in a hollow. Incubation 21–28 days; fledging 4 weeks. One brood.

Dove, rock   *Columba livia*

Resident, but decreasing in numbers and hopelessly interbred with its own descendants, the domestic pigeon. The only pure rock doves that remain are probably to be found on the north and west coasts of Scotland and Ireland. Rocky sea cliffs and coastal fields.

Nests in seacaves or among rocks at wilder parts of coast. Few bits of heather or roots in a hole or cave ledge or crevice.

Nestbox: This species was domesticated hundreds of years ago (see page 83). The flourishing domesticated forms (feral pigeons) have confused

Pigeons like to nest sociably.

125

the wild status of the bird in no uncertain terms. But whether you are dealing with street pigeons or fantails the principles of nestboxing are the same. Pigeons are happiest in a dark chamber which recalls the cave crevices of their ancestors. A garden dovecot, round or octagonal, should be mounted on a stout pole to discourage cats and rats. A two-storey structure makes sense, allowing a number of pairs to breed in companionable proximity. The 'pigeon holes' should provide chambers roughly 24 in × 18 in × 18 in (60 cm × 45 cm × 45 cm) high, with an entrance hole 6 in × 6 in (15 cm × 15 cm). The house should be draught free, but well ventilated, and there should be a generous landing shelf outside the entrance holes (unlike blue tits, pigeons *do* like to land outside the entrance). A roof should keep rain off and also slope south, providing a warm place for the birds to sunbathe and posture.

Eggs: 2 white. April onwards. Incubation 17–19 days; fledging 4–5 weeks. Two or three broods, maybe more.

Dove, stock   *Columba oenas*
Resident and well distributed, except in northern Scotland. Open parkland, wooded country, cliffs and sand dunes.

Nests in holes in old trees, rocks, rabbit burrows, buildings. Insubstantial structure of few twigs, bits of grass, or nothing at all.

Nestbox: Enclosed, with 8 in (20 cm) diameter entrance hole, 15 in (38 cm) interior depth, 15 in × 25 in (38 cm × 63.5 cm) floor. May take to a tree-mounted kestrel box.

Eggs: 2 creamy-white. Incubation 16–18 days; fledging 28 days. Three, four or even five broods.

Owl, barn   *Tyto alba*
Resident, generally distributed but not abundant and decreasing. Vicinity of farms, old buildings, church towers, etc. Parkland with old timber.

Nests in ruins or unoccupied buildings, hollow trees and cliff crevices. No material used, the eggs are often surrounded by a pile of cast pellets.

Nestbox: Barn owls are a beneficial species from the point of view of farmers, hunting a diet of short tailed voles, common shrews and wood mice. Formerly much persecuted by the ignorant, they have been further declining in this century because of habitat loss and human disturbance. But there is also a chronic shortage of suitable nest sites such as old trees, derelict buildings and old-style brick and timber barns. The modern steel-framed barns offer no home to nesting barn owls. Fortunately, they take

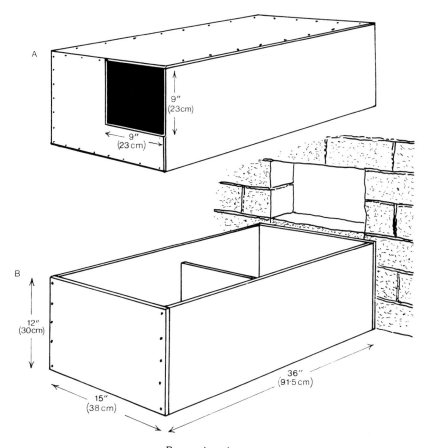

Barn owl nestboxes.
Type A should be used in timber-trussed or modern steel-framed barns.
Type B is for enclosed storage barns with access from the outside.

readily to nestboxes, particularly if the box is placed in a building which is not too often disturbed.

There are several designs, and it may be necessary to use a good deal of ingenuity in fitting the box to the site. The RSPB suggests that enclosed storage barns with access from outside are most favoured, but open Dutch barns are also suitable, particularly if the nestbox can be secured to beams or struts and used for roosting in winter. This will increase the chance of nesting the following year.

The design of the boxes is quite straightforward, as they can easily be made from a standard tea chest or packing case – both for lightness and ease of conversion they are hard to beat. If you can find a source of supply,

127

wooden barrels are also easy to convert. Tea chests and packing cases, however, are not waterproof and should only be sited in dry locations. If the nestboxes are exposed to the elements, more durable and water-resistant material must be used. The lining papers and metal edging around the top of the chest must be removed and any nails knocked flat. You will also need some wooden trays – baker's trays are ideal – which are sawn in half to provide two platforms of about 18 in (45 cm) in depth. These are important as they provide a safe area in front of the box where the young can come out and stretch their wings.

It is easiest to erect a nestbox in a timber barn – a steel-trussed building may require considerable ingenuity. The most important parts to remember are that the boxes must be secure inside the barn, as high above the ground as possible, in the darkest corner out of any draughts and where there is permanent access for the birds. Since height is one of the main criteria, the easiest time for putting up the boxes is when the barn is full of bales. In a timber-trussed barn the box is first nailed, from the inside, front and back to the beam with 3 in nails to give a firm fixing. The front which has already had a 9 in × 9 in (23 cm × 23 cm) opening cut out of the corner, is then fixed to the open end with 1 in nails. Finally, the tray is nailed in front of the box. In some cases, it may be necessary to support the platform on timber runners nailed to the underside of the box.

If the barn has steel roof trusses, it is best to nail vertical and horizontal pieces of timber to the box; these can be firmly roped, wired or G-cramped to the steelwork. Every ounce of ingenuity should be used when dealing with these barns, as very often they are the only suitable roosting and nesting-sites for miles around. Boxes can also be placed in corner sites and hung from ridge purlins, but virtually every barn demands its own solution. Barrels can be placed in disused lofts, but here access must be restricted while the birds are nesting.

Whether your boxes are occupied or not, keep the knowledge of their whereabouts restricted to as few as possible. Human predation is, unfortunately, a reality as is disturbance by well-meaning but misguided birdwatchers. Never let any unwanted eyes see you checking a building and only visit occasionally, preferably towards dusk, so that if the adult is inadvertently flushed, it will quickly return. A most important point is that the barn owl is included on Schedule 1 of the Bird Protection Act. This means that both the bird and its eggs are specially protected by law, and if you intend to visit your occupied nestboxes you must obtain a special Government Permit. If you see that the box is occupied early in the breeding season, it is probably best to watch from a safe distance, thus avoiding disturbing the birds and the need to become involved in such legalities. The Bird Protection Laws do not hinder the farmer from going about his normal business using the barn!

Eggs: 4–7 white. March to July. Incubation 32–34 days; fledging about 10 weeks. Frequently two broods.

Owl, little   *Athene noctua*

Little owls were first introduced to Britain from Italy by Charles Waterton, in May 1842, though it was some thirty years later that a similar experiment was successful in the long term. Lack of suitable tree holes may be one of the reasons for their current decline. Resident in southern half of England.

Nests in trees, farm-building holes and rabbit burrows.

Nestbox: Enclosed, at least 4 in (10 cm) diameter entrance hole, inside depth 12 in (30 cm), floor 8 in × 8 in (20 cm × 20 cm). Also may use kestrel

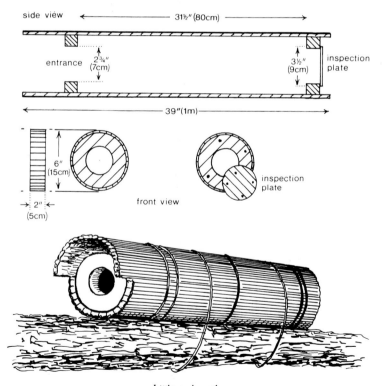

Little owl nestbox.

box. One of the most successful designs is the 'hollow branch'. Take two round, equal-sized wooden discs of softwood, approximately 2 in (5 cm) thick and not less than 6 in (15 cm) diameter. Bore a $2\frac{3}{4}$ in (70 mm) entrance hole in one disc. Form a drum by nailing wooden slats 39 in × 1 in × $\frac{1}{2}$ in (1 m × 25 mm × 12.5 mm) to the discs which should be $31\frac{1}{2}$ in (80 cm) apart. Secure the drum with wire and wrap it with a layer of roofing felt. Camouflage with a layer of rush mat or loose bark and fasten with wire. Mount on a thick horizontal branch some 10 ft to 16 ft (3 m to 5 m) high, the drum sloping slightly to the rear. Don't expose the entrance to the prevailing wind. Prime with garden peat. It is important that the interior is not less than $31\frac{1}{2}$ in (80 cm) long and the closed end must be light-proof.

Eggs: 3–5 white. April and May. Incubation 28–29 days; fledging about 26 days. Usually one brood.

Owl, tawny   *Strix aluco*
Resident and generally distributed in Britain, but never recorded wild in Ireland. Woodland, farmland, parks and well timbered gardens.

Nests in tree holes, second-hand crow, hawk and heron nests, squirrel dreys. Sometimes in barns and on rocky ledges. Branch may need sawing above hole to prevent loss of nest site due to gales.

Nestbox: Enclosed with 8 in (20 cm) diameter hole at top (see drawing), inside depth 30 in (76 cm), floor 8 in × 8 in (20 cm × 20 cm). Will use a barrel (40 gallon best, 6 gallon has been used successfully), if a hole is opened in it and the barrel fixed to a tree crutch about 12 ft to 30 ft (3.6 m to 9 m) high, although the height is probably not critical.

The chimney type nestbox (see drawing) has four wooden planks at least 30 in (76 cm) long and 8 in (20 cm) wide butted onto each other, using 2 in or $2\frac{1}{2}$ in oval nails, to make a square-sectioned chimney. A 9 in × 9 in (23 cm × 23 cm) base which must be perforated by at least half a dozen drainage holes, is nailed to one end to form the floor. A thin sheet of ferrous metal is to be preferred to either perforated zinc or a wooden floor. A layer of dry peat or sawdust should be added to the completed base to counteract the fouling that will occur in the fledging period. Chimney boxes of this size are too deep for a hand to reach to the bottom, either for examining, or ringing the nestlings, or for cleaning out. It is practical to make an observation door on one side of the box 8 in × 6 in (20 cm × 15 cm), which is hinged to the back of the box and fastened at the front by a hook-and-eye catch. Fit the box under a lateral tree bough at an angle of about 30° from the vertical. If attaching to main trunk, contrive an angle of about 45° to simulate a broken

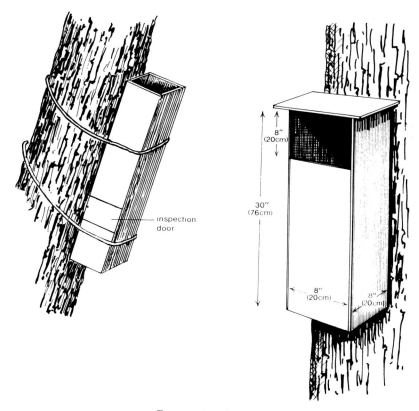

inspection door

8" (20cm)

30" (76cm)

8" (20cm)

8" (20cm)

Tawny owl nestboxes.

branch. Secure to the tree by wire bands at both top and bottom, but remember these will rust through, or become embedded in bark, so watch your maintenance.

Eggs: 2–4 white. February to early April. Incubation 28–30 days; fledging about 4 weeks. One brood.

Owl, long-eared *Asio otus*

Locally distributed over most of British Isles, least common in south-west. Mainly in coniferous woods, plantations, shelter belts; also in well-ivied deciduous woods and marshes, dunes, moorland with low bushes.

Nests in second-hand crow, sparrowhawk, pigeon or heron nests.

Nestbox: Has been known to use duck-type nest baskets in Holland.

Eggs: 4–5 white. March, early April. Incubation 27–28 days; fledging about 23 days. One brood.

131

Swift *Apus apus*

Summer resident, generally distributed except in north-west Scotland, arriving late April, early May, leaving early August. Habitat exclusively aerial. Rarely on ground except at nest.

Nests in colonies, under eaves, in crevices and in holes. Bits of straw, grass, feathers, seed fluff, collected on the wing and stuck together with saliva to form a cup.

Nestbox: Using a plank 65 in × 8 in × $\frac{3}{4}$ in (165 cm × 20 cm × 10 mm), make a box 19½ in × 8 in × 5½ in (49.5 cm × 20 cm × 14 cm) with an entrance hole cut in the *floor* of the box (not the end, as swifts prefer to enter vertically from below). Make box longer than 19½ in (49.5 cm) if convenient,

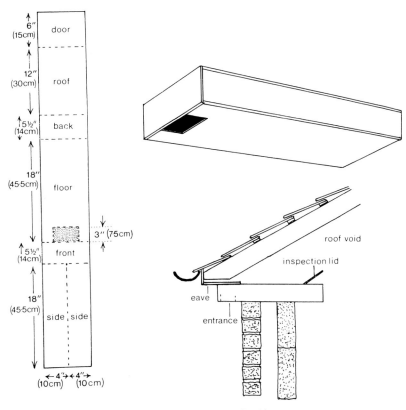

Swift nestbox in place on side of house.
By removing a brick or section of wood from the eaves the box may be positioned within the loft with only the entrance hole visible from outside.

but not shorter, as they like to nest at least 1 ft (30 cm) from the entrance hole. Prime nest area with a ring of twisted straw. Cut an inspection door 6 in × 8 in (15 cm × 20 cm) at rear roof to aid cleaning. Site it under the eaves at least 12 ft (3.6 m) above ground, up to 100 ft (30 m) if necessary. Block entrance hole till swifts first arrive, at the end of April or the beginning of May, in order to discourage earlier nesting sparrows and starlings.

Alternative plan: Open out a narrow slit in eaves to allow entrance to roof of your house.

Eggs: 2 or 3 white. Late May, early June. Incubation 18–19 days; fledging about 6 weeks. One brood.

Kingfisher *Alcedo atthis*

Resident and generally distributed, except in Scotland. Streams, rivers, canals, lakes, estuaries (especially in winter).

Nests in tunnels in banks of streams or sand pits, boring 2 in (5 cm) tunnels as far as 4 ft (1.2 m) to a nest chamber, preferably in sandy soil.

Artificial nest-site: Will excavate tunnel in artificial bank by suitable stream, a procedure developed by Ron and Rose Eastman. Fix fencing posts eg willow, which will sprout even if embedded in concrete. Stretch $2\frac{1}{2}$ in (63 mm) mesh chicken wire or square mesh pig wire, to a height of 4ft (1.2 m) or more to make a vertical face, facing north if possible, with a degree of privacy and foliage. Fill in behind wire wall with sand or sandy soil. Provide perches and posts nearby. There is no need to cut entrance hole in the netting. The Wildfowl Trust at Arundel in Sussex have had success with this design.

Eggs: 6–7 white. Late April to August. Incubation 19–21 days; fledging 23–27 days. Two, three or even more broods.

Hoopoe *Upupa epops*

Passage migrant, regular in small numbers in spring, less frequent in autumn, on south, south-east and south-west coasts and in east coast as far north as Norfolk. Rare elsewhere in Great Britain. Open woodland, orchards, parkland.

Nests in tree holes, crevices and holes in rough stone walls and ruins. Rarely in southern coastal counties.

Nestboxes: Use large nestboxes on the continent.

Eggs: 5–8 whitish-grey or yellowish-olive. May and June. Incubation 18 days; fledging 20–27 days. Two broods.

Wryneck *Jynx torquilla*

Summer resident. Decreasing and scarce in south-east England with a very few pairs now left. However, there are signs of influx to Scotland from Scandinavia, with birds breeding in the Spey Valley, for example.

Nestbox: Improve a tree hole. Or try an enclosed box, with a $\frac{3}{8}$ in × $1\frac{3}{4}$ in (10 mm × 45 mm) diameter entrance, a 6 in (15 cm) interior depth, and a 5 in × 5 in (12.7 cm × 12.7 cm) floor.

Eggs: 7–10 white. End of May till July. Incubation 12 days; fledging 19–21 days. Usually one brood.

Woodpecker, green *Picus viridis*

Resident but local in England and Wales, rare in Scotland, none in Ireland. Deciduous woods, park and farmland.

Nests in tree trunks, choosing soft or rotting timber, boring a hole horizontally 2 in to 3 in (5.0 cm to 7.5 cm) then descending to make a nest compartment over 1 ft (30 cm) deep and about 6 in (15 cm) wide at its broadest. Put a few chips at the bottom to form the nest. Sometimes, old holes are used again. Often, starlings take over from them.

Nestbox: Enclosed type with $2\frac{1}{2}$ in (63 mm) entrance hole, interior depth 15 in (38 cm), floor 5 in × 5 in (12.7 cm × 12.7 cm). Ideal for starlings!

Eggs: 5–7 translucent. End of April to May. Incubation 18–19 days; fledging 18–21 days. One brood.

Martin, sand *Riparia riparia*

Summer resident, widely distributed. Open country with water.

Nests colonially, digging a long tunnel to a nest chamber, in sand and gravel pits, railway cuttings, river banks and sea cliffs. Few grasses and feathers.

Try boring a few enticing 2 in (5 cm) diameter holes in likely sandbanks, steep road cuttings and banks, especially over water – they may use drainage pipes in a wall which can be deliberately placed for them. A few score breed in this sort of location at the RSPB's Minsmere Reserve in Suffolk, at the car park.

Nestboxes: Near an existing colony, it is worth preparing some underground chambers. Dig a vertical shaft 1 ft (30 cm) deep, line it with boxing, arrange an access tunnel 2 in (5 cm) square, from the vertical cliff entrance. The length of the horizontal passage is not critical. Close the nest chamber with a removable lid 6 in (15 cm) from the floor. Close roof of the shaft with another lid which is concealed by a turf.

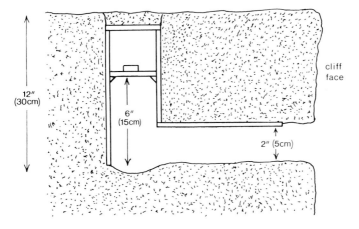

Sand martin nestbox.

Eggs: 4–5 white. Mid May onwards. Incubation 14 days; fledging 19 days. Two broods.

Swallow *Hirundo rustica*

Summer resident, generally distributed. Open farmland, meadows, ponds.

Nests on rafts and joists, building open mud-and-straw cup, lined with grasses and feathers.

Nestbox: Improvise a simple saucer shape, or fix half a coconut or a 4 in × 4 in (10 cm × 10 cm) shallow tray to joist or rafter, even as low as 6 ft (1.8 m). Will also use specially adapted house martin nestbox placed singly *inside* building. Or, using an old nest, make a plaster of paris mould of the interior. Then take potting clay to make a thick replica, complete with fixing flanges or saddles to fit over a joist, remembering that swallows like to nest against something. Remember to allow continuous access to the nest-site.

Eggs: 4–5 white, spotted with red-brown. Mid May till October. Incubation 15 days; fledging 3 weeks. Usually two broods.

Martin, house *Delichon urbica*

Summer resident, generally distributed.

Originally a cliff nester, has now adopted buildings. Nests colonially on outside walls, under eaves. Cup shape made of mud gobbets with feathers.

Nestbox: Artificial nest from Nerine Nurseries (for address see page 181). Fix under eaves or high window sill. For best results an existing house

135

martin colony should be close at hand. One nest may work, but the more the merrier. Put them in groups outside, under the horizontal or sloping eaves of houses, barns, etc. The artificial cups are held in position by cup-hooks so that it is possible to slide the nest freely in and out to inspect the contents. The entrance hole for house martin nest cups should be no more than 1 in (25 mm) deep, in order to exclude sparrows. Nevertheless, there have been cases where the hole has been enlarged and sparrows have gained access. There is a method which has been successful in stopping this, based on the fact that martins are able to approach a nest at a much steeper angle than sparrows (see drawing page 137). The hanging cords of the curtain should be no more than 12 in (30 cm) long and should be fixed to hang 6 in (15 cm) away from the entrance hole. A spacing of 2½ in (63 mm) between the cords is effective. Use ⅞ in steel nuts as weights on the cord ends. Have all the cords the same length so that they are less likely to tangle in a wind.

One of the objects of using artificial nests is that they frequently encourage house martins to adopt a house not previously 'tenanted' and make their own nests. So, even if the boxes are not used, they may be successful in their purpose. But single nests away from an existing colony are susceptible to attack from sparrows. If the birds try to build and the nests fall off the eaves, a series of nails in the facia board may help with their adhesion.

Eggs: 4–5 white. Late May to October. Incubation 14–15 days; fledging 19–21 days. Usually two broods, often three.

Wagtail, pied *Motacilla alba*
Resident and generally distributed. Gardens, farms, buildings and cultivated country.

Nests in holes and on ledges of walls, outhouses, creeper, banks and cliffs. Leaves, twigs, stems, lined with hair, wool and feathers.

Nestbox: Ledge or open fronted box, with a floor area of not less than 4 in × 4 in (10 cm × 10 cm). Fix it in a stone wall. Or make a cavity behind a loose stone which can be used as an inspection door.

Eggs: 5–6 greyish- or bluish-white, spotted grey-brown and grey. Late April to June. Incubation 13–14 days; fledging 14–15 days. Two broods. Often host to cuckoo.

Dipper *Cinclus cinclus*
Resident, generally distributed in suitable localities. Fast-flowing streams and rivers of hills and mountainous regions.

Nests in wall and bridge holes, rock faces, tree roots and under waterfalls, always close to fast-moving water. Construction of mosses, grasses under an overhang.

Nestbox: May occasionally occupy an open fronted robin-type box. A German design has been developed to provide nest recesses in the supports for concrete bridges at the time of construction. The essence of the operation is that a recess (see drawing) is left in the concrete by making a mould which is filled with expanded polystyrene and then inserted into the mould for the concrete bridge section. Once the concrete has set, the entrance hole is chipped out and the polystyrene removed. The only remaining task is to fit a front section over the opening. Arrange a suitable perch or dipping stone just above water level if there isn't one already.

Eggs: About 5 white. End of March. Incubation about 16 days; fledging 19–25 days. Usually two broods.

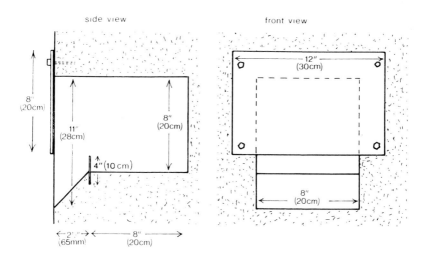

Nest recess for dippers.

Wren *Troglodytes troglodytes*

Resident and generally distributed. Gardens, thickets, woods, rock banks. Avoids the centres of large towns.

137

Nests in hedges, holes in trees, banks or buildings. Cock bird makes several nests of moss, grass, leaves, etc, and the hen lines her choice with feathers sometimes weeks after the male built it.

Nestbox: May take to a tit box, but is much more likely to find a natural or semi-natural place such as a faggot pile or creeper-clad wall. Excavate a cavity in a bundle of pea sticks or brushwood and lean it against a wall. Provide a coil of rope in the corner of a shed, or hang up an old coat with capacious pocket.

Eggs: 5–6 white, spotted with brownish red. Incubation 14–15 days; fledging 16–17 days. Usually two broods.

Robin *Erithacus rubecula*

Resident and generally distributed, except in extreme north of Scotland. Gardens, hedgerows, woods with undergrowth.

Nests in gardens and hedgerows in bankside hollows, tree holes, walls, amongst creeper, on shelves in outbuildings, often at foot of bush or grassy tuft. Foundation of dried leaves and moss, neatly lined with hair and perhaps a feather or two.

Nestbox: Ledge or tray, open-fronted box. Interior floor at least 4 in × 4 in (10 cm × 10 cm). Old tin, watering can, or kettle, at least quart-size, well shaded from sun, spout down for drainage. Fix it about 5 in (1.5 m) up in a strong fork site. Prime with a plaited circle of straw.

Eggs: Usually 5–6 white, with sandy or reddish freckles. Late March to July. Incubation 13–14 days; fledging 12–14 days. Two or more broods.

Redstart *Phoenicurus phoenicurus*

Summer resident, widely distributed but local. Woodland, parks, bushy commons with old trees, ruins, orchards, well-timbered gardens.

Nests in holes such as tree or stump, building, walls, outhouses, rocks, quarries. Nest made of grass, strips of bark, mosses, roots, and lined with hair and feathers.

Nestbox: Enclosed with entrance hole $1\frac{1}{8}$ in to 2 in (29 mm to 50 mm) diameter, inside depth not less than 5 in (12.5 cm), and floor not less than 4 in × 4 in (10 cm × 10 cm). Make sure there is a perch not far away from the box (but not on it).

Eggs: About 6 pale blue. May onwards. Incubation 14 days; fledging 14 days. Sometimes two broods.

Traditional kettle nest for robins. Make sure the
spout points downwards so that rainwater drains away.

Wheatear   *Oenanthe oenanthe*

Summer visitor, locally common in open country, loose boulders and scree,
rabbit warrens, moorland, highland roads, chalk downs, sandy commons
and sand dunes, stony shores, rocky islands.

Nests under a boulder or stone, in rabbit burrow or stone wall. Grass and
moss, linings of rabbit fur, feathers, wool.

Nestbox: Has nested under tin cans and in tunnel-type prefabs made of
bricks sunk in the shingle at Dungeness Bird Observatory. Be careful to
protect the chamber from excessive sunshine, by piling soil or gravel over
any metal parts.

Eggs: Usually 6 pale blue. Late April or May. Incubation 14 days; fledging
about 15 days. One brood.

139

Blackbird *Turdus merula*

Resident and generally distributed. Woods, hedges, gardens, shrubberies.

Nests in hedges, bushes, evergreens, ivy, sometimes in outhouses. Sturdily built of grasses, roots, etc. Inner mud cup lined with grasses.

Nestbox: Tray or open-fronted, with a floor area 12 in × 12 in (30 cm × 30 cm). Or try an inverted cone made of roofing felt. Cut into circle 9 in (23 cm) in diameter. Cut out and reject a V-shaped sector from centre to a 2 in (5 cm) arc at periphery. Cut a 1 in (2.5 cm) section from centre (to provide drainage). Now overlap open ends 3 in (7.5 cm) and staple strongly. Resulting cone is approx 7 in (17.5 cm) in diameter with a depth of 2 in (5 cm). Or try a bundle of pea sticks arranged with a central cave.

Eggs: 4–5 bluish-green, freckled with red-brown. February (or even earlier) to July. Incubation 13–14 days; fledging 13–14 days. Two or three broods, the first often being vandalised because it is insufficiently concealed by leaves, later broods being more successful. Five broods have been raised in one season.

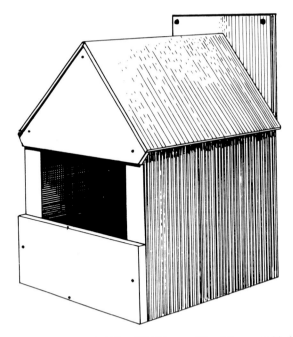

Open-type nestbox with 12″ × 12″ (30 cm × 30 cm) floor, suitable for blackbird. A smaller version may be used by robins or spotted flycatchers, but open boxes are usually less successful than the enclosed versions, since natural open nest-sites are more plentiful than holes in trees.

Flycatcher, spotted   *Muscicapa striata*

Summer resident, generally distributed. Gardens, parks, woodland edges.

Nests against wall or on small ledge supported by creeper or fruit trees, etc. Moss and grass, lined with wool, hair or feathers.

Nestbox: Ledge or open fronted box with at least 3 in × 3 in (7.5 cm × 7.5 cm) floor. Hide one of those bowl-shaped wire flower baskets in dense honeysuckle, primed with some moss. Have a perch not far away.

Eggs: 4–5 greenish-grey, with brown spots. Mid May to June. Incubation 12–13; fledging 12–13 days. One brood.

Spotted flycatcher at nest in plant basket.

Flycatcher, pied   *Muscicapa hypoleuca*

Summer resident but rather local and absent from south-east England. Particularly in oakwoods and alder and birch woods along rivers or streams.

Nests in holes of trees, walls. Bark, leaves, grasses with a lining of fibres and grass.

141

Nestbox: Enclosed, with entrance hole 1⅛ in to 2 in (29 mm to 50 mm) in diameter, inside depth not less than 5 in (12.5 cm), floor not less than 4 in × 4 in (10 cm × 10 cm). Have a convenient perch close to the nestbox, but not on it. Takes readily to boxes, which seem to supply a real need.

Eggs: 4–9 pale blue. Mid May. Incubation 12–13 days; fledging 13 days. One brood.

Tit, marsh   *Parus palustris*

Resident and widespread in most of England and Wales, but not Scotland or Ireland. Deciduous woods, hedgerows, thickets and sometimes in gardens. Likes to be near woodland and not, as might be imagined, marshes.

Nests in holes in willows, alders, sometimes in walls. Moss with lining of hair or down.

Nestbox: As blue tit.

Eggs: 7–8 white, spotted red-brown. End April and May. Incubation 13 days; fledging 16–17 days. Generally one brood.

Tit, willow   *Parus atricapillus*

Resident. Fairly frequent in parts of south-east England, scattered locally elsewhere. Marshy or damp woods, hedges and thickets.

Excavates a nest chamber in soft rotten wood – usually birch, willow, alder or elder. Pad of down mixed with wood-fibre, some feathers.

Nestbox: As for blue tit, but not enthusiastic. Stuff it full of sawdust so that the willow tit has to excavate a hole. But a far more successful method is to get a rotten silver birch or alder trunk about 6 ft (1.8 m) long and 5 in or 6 in (12.5 cm or 15 cm) in diameter, and strap it to a convenient tree, allowing the bird to finish the job. Cap the top with polythene so that rain cannot penetrate easily. It seems that the presence of a suitable rotten tree which they can excavate is all that is needed to attract them to breed in an area they visit during winter. Nests are usually between 2 ft and 5 ft (60 cm and 1.5 cm) high, averaging 3 ft (90 cm), so place the trunk accordingly. Birch is the preferred site, alder and elder are a poor second.

Eggs: 8 or 9 white, spotted brown-red. Late April and May. Incubation 13 days; fledging 17–19 days. Probably one brood.

Tit, crested   *Parus cristatus*

Resident in a few parts of north-east Scotland only. Pine forests and woods.

Nests in holes or crevices in old and decayed pine stumps, also in alders and birches and sometimes in fencing posts. Dead moss lined with hair of deer or hare, sometimes feathers or wool.

Nestbox: Enclosed, with 1⅛ in to 1½ in (29 mm to 38 mm) entrance hole, interior depth not less than 5 in (12.5 cm), floor not less than 4 in × 4 in (10 cm × 10 cm)

Eggs: 5–6 white, splotched with chestnut red. End April and May. Incubation 14–15 days; fledging 17–18 days. One brood.

Blue tit with nestlings.

Tit, coal *Parus ater*

Resident and generally distributed. Wooded country and gardens with a preference for conifers. Not so commonly found in orchards and hedgerows.

Nests in tree, wall or bank holes, close to ground. Moss with thick layer of hair or down and feathers.

Nestbox: As blue tit.

Eggs: 7–11 white, with reddish-brown spots. Late April and May. Incubation 17–18 days; fledging 16 days. Sometimes two broods but usually in different nestboxes.

Tit, blue   *Parus caeruleus*

Resident and generally distributed except in north-west Scotland. Woodland, hedges, gardens.

Nests as great tit. Blue tits may go to a nestbox because the best natural sites have been taken by the dominant great tits.

Nestbox: Enclosed, with 1 in to 1¾ in (25 mm to 30 mm) entrance hole, otherwise as great tit.

Eggs: 7–14 (though there is a record of 19!), usually spotted light chestnut. Late April and May. Incubation 13–14 days; fledging 15–21 days. One brood. Blue tits breed most successfully in deciduous woodland, where there is an abundance of caterpillars. Their breeding success is least in built-up areas, even though their clutch sizes are smaller to compensate for the poor food available.

Tit, great   *Parus major*

Resident and generally distributed, scarcer in northern Scotland. Woodland, hedges, gardens.

Nests in tree or wall holes, or crevices. Also in second-hand nests, or the foundations of larger nests. If no natural sites are available, it may use letterboxes, flower pots, beehives and almost any kind of hole. Nest lined with a thick layer of hair or down.

Nestbox: Enclosed, with 1⅛ in (29 mm) diameter entrance hole or slightly larger, interior depth at least 5 in (12.5 cm) from hole to floor, and floor at least 4 in × 4 in (10 cm × 10 cm). Great tits are the most enthusiastic customers for boxes, with blue tits coming second. They not uncommonly occupy the same box, the great tits taking over, covering the blue tits' eggs with a fresh lining and hatching only their own eggs (though mixed broods are not unknown). Tit boxes are successful even in woodland, where there is a shortage of old trees because management procedures do not tolerate them. Result is strong competition for sites.

Eggs: 5–11 white, splotched reddish brown. End April to June. Incubation 13–14 days; fledging about 3 weeks. One brood.

144

Nuthatch *Sitta europae*

Resident and fairly common in Wales and southern England. Old trees in woods, parkland, gardens.

Nests in tree holes or sometimes in wall hole. Female fills crevice and reduces entrance to desired size with mud. Nest lined with flakes of bark or leaves.

Nestbox: Enclosed, with $1\frac{1}{8}$ in to $1\frac{1}{2}$ in (29 mm to 38 mm) entrance hole, interior depth not less than 5 in, floor not less than 4 in × 4 in (10 cm × 10 cm).

Eggs: 5–9 white, spotted with red-brown. End April to June. Incubation 14–15 days; fledging about 24. One brood.

Nuthatches plaster their entrance holes with mud.

145

Tree creeper *Certhia familiaris*

Resident and generally distributed. Woodland, parks, gardens with large trees.

Nests behind loose bark or cracks on tree trunks, or behind ivy. Sometimes in wall or building crevices. Twigs, moss, grass, lined with feathers and bits of wool.

Nestbox: May come to conventional enclosed type, but a wedge-shaped box has been specially designed with their needs in mind (see below). An alternative design involves a book-shaped box 7¼ in (18 cm) tall by 4¾ in × 1⁹⁄₁₆ in (12 cm × 4 cm), with a 2 in × 1 in (5 cm × 2.5 cm) entrance hole at

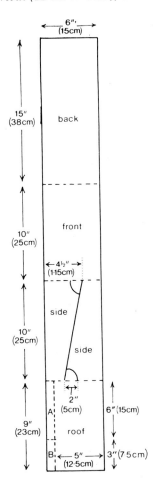

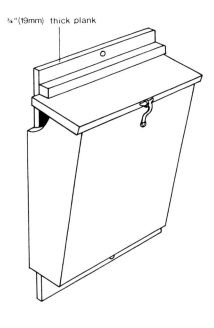

Tree creeper nestbox. In the cutting diagram the stops A and B are attached to the back A and the roof B with impact adhesive. The loose roof is fastened to the front with a brass hook and eye.

the top of the 'spine'. Clamp it to a tree trunk at around 10 ft (3 m) high. Or try securing a loose piece of bark to a tree trunk to simulate a natural crevice.

Eggs: Usually white, with red-brown spots at larger end. End April to June. Incubation 14–15 days; fledging 14–15 days. There may be a second brood.

Chough *Pyrrhocorax pyrrhocorax*

Resident but hard pressed, less than a thousand breeding pairs left in the British Isles, confined to Scotland, Wales and Ireland.

Nests in crevices or holes in cliffs and sea caves. Bulky structure of sticks, heather stalks, etc, lined with wool and hair.

Has been known to use artificial covered nest sites in ruins and such places as Martello towers.

Eggs: 3 or 4 blue with brown spots. Late April onwards. Incubation 17–18 days; fledging about 38 days. One brood.

Even the rare chough may use an artificial nest site.

147

Jackdaw   *Corvus monedula*
Resident and common except in north-west Scotland. Farm and parkland, cliffs, old buildings.

Nests in colonies in trees, buildings, rocks or rabbit burrows, holes, cracks or crevices. Almost any hole will do – often in bottom of rook or heron's nest. Twigs, sometimes very bulky, sometimes not. Lining of grass, wool, hair, etc.

Nestbox: Enclosed type, with not less than 6 in (15 cm) entrance hole, 17 in (43 cm) interior depth, and at least a $7\frac{1}{2} \times 7\frac{1}{2}$ in (19 cm × 19 cm) floor. Or open type as for kestrel.

Eggs: Usually 4–6 pale greenish-blue, spotted brownish black. Mid April. Incubation 17–18 days; fledging 17–18 days. One brood.

Starling   *Sturnus vulgaris*
Resident and generally distributed. Found almost anywhere, having successfully adapted to man's ways.

Nests, often in colonies, in tree or building holes. Untidy structure of straw and grasses lined with feathers.

Nestbox: Enclosed, with entrance hole 2 in (5 cm) diameter, inside depth 12 in (30 cm), floor area 9 in × 9 in (23 cm × 23 cm). Starlings will explore many possibilities of piracy, and will sometimes take over an *old* tit box, when the wood has softened enough to enable them to hack away at the hole and enlarge it. If they annoy you by taking over the nestbox, consider that there may be a great spotted woodpecker nearby who has been spared eviction.

Eggs: 5–7 pale blue. End of March onwards. (They often get taken short and lay one on the lawn.) Incubation 12–13 days; fledging 20–22 days. Usually one brood, two in south-east England.

Sparrow, house   *Passer domesticus*
Resident and widely distributed. Cultivated land and vicinity of human habitation.

Nests in holes or niches around occupied houses: eaves, drainpiping, creeper, also in hedges and trees, house martins' nests, or in the foundations of rooks' nests. Untidy structure of straw and grasses lined with feathers and oddments. In cramped locations may consist of lining only.

Nestbox: Enclosed, with entrance hole $1\frac{1}{4}$ in (32 mm) diameter, inside depth not less than 5 in (12.5 cm), floor area 6 in × 6 in (15 cm × 15 cm).

148

May easily become a pest, denying nestboxes to more welcome birds. Drastic solution is to destroy nests as soon as they are built.

Eggs: 3–5 greyish-white, finely spotted grey and brown. May to August. Incubation 12–14 days; fledging 15 days. Two to three broods.

House sparrows are expert at taking over nestboxes which may have been provided with different species in mind.

Sparrow, tree *Passer montanus*

Resident and widely distributed in England, Wales, eastern side of Scotland and a few parts of Ireland. 'Country cousin' of house sparrow, frequenting same habitat but less attached to human habitations.

149

Nests in holes of trees, banks, haystacks and thatch, buildings and in foundations of disused rook or magpie nests. Untidy, similar to that of house sparrow.

Nestbox: Enclosed, with entrance hole 1⅛ in (28 mm) diameter, inside depth not less than 6 in (15.25 cm), floor not less than 4 in × 4 in (10 cm × 10 cm).

Eggs: 4–6, smaller, browner, darker than those of house sparrow. Late April to August. Incubation 12–14 days; fledging 12–14 days. Two broods usually.

FIVE
Bathing and drinking

A healthy bird gets most of its water requirements from its food, but it still needs access to a supply of clean fresh water, partly because it will drink a little, but mainly because it bathes a lot. Birds don't sweat. If they get overheated they open their mouths wide and gape to lose heat, thus losing some moisture, but they also lose moisture by excretion and this must be replaced. Some species are adapted to a minimal water intake. Desert birds like the budgerigar can go for long periods without drinking even though they are living on a dry diet of seeds. However, don't deprive your caged budgies of water on this basis! Tree-living species may sip from foliage after rain, and for this reason there may be some sense in providing a drinking

Song thrush sun bathing. In this typical posture the bird is naturally hot, so it is gaping to lose moisture.

bowl well off the ground. Many town birds happily visit roof gutters to drink and to bathe.

Most birds drink by dipping their bills into the water, then raising their heads to allow the liquid to run down their throats. But pigeons keep their bills in the water, sucking it up and into the system in bulk, a method which is quick and leaves the bird at risk for the shortest time. Swallows, martins and swifts will drink in flight in a shower of rain, or from the surface of the pond. And, like other birds, they enjoy bathing in rain or even flying through the spray of a lawn sprinkler. However, they will be cautious of bathing in a downpour, since the object of bathing is to wet the plumage but not to soak it.

The function of bathing is to maintain the bird's plumage in tip-top condition, mainly because of its importance in flight and thermal insulation. Birds need to bathe even in the depths of winter, since ill-kept plumage will not serve the purpose of keeping warmth in and cold out. Birds, like mammals, are warm-blooded creatures, maintaining a high and constant metabolic rate. Their body temperature is kept up by internally generated heat, as opposed to the system endured by reptiles and fishes whose body temperatures fluctuate in sympathy with that of the ambient environment.

The bathing process, in birds, is highly ritualised. First the plumage is made wet, but not too wet. (Caught in a heavy downpour of rain, birds will hunch and stretch up, so that the water runs off quickly.) Next, the excess

Robin bathing.

drops are shaken off before the oiling stage begins. Twisting its tail to one side, the bird reaches its bill back to collect fatty oil from the preen gland on its rump. The oil is then carefully smeared all over its feathers, the difficult job of oiling the head being carried out by using the feet. After oiling, which is characteristically an urgent process, comes the more leisurely task of preening, the final stage of the ritual, where the bird nibbles and strokes its feathers, one by one, into shape. It then stretches and settles for a period of contemplation.

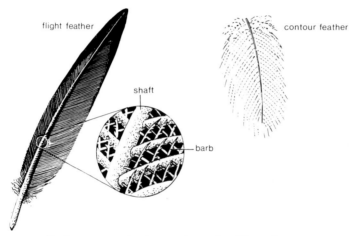

Feathers are complex devices, designed in different forms to serve different functions—thermal insulation, waterproofing and surface protection, flight capability and display.

Feathers are an engineeering marvel, precisely designed for their several tasks of flight, control, aerodynamic contouring and thermal insulation, to say nothing of the advertising display function which is such an important part of their courtship. A long, tapered central shaft – the rachis – supports a sheet of interlocking barbs and barbules on the vanes. The vanes are symmetrical, either side of the rachis, in the case of body feathers whose function is to retain warmth and provide shaping, but asymmetrical in the primary flight feathers. In their case, the rachis is located near to the leading edge, which is stiffer and thicker than the trailing edge, thus improving the aerofoil section. By the same token, while the central tail feather has symmetrically balanced vanes, the rachis is placed progressively nearer the outboard side of the vanes on the side tail feathers.

Birds do not only bathe in water. On occasions they will enjoy sun, rain, snow, smoke and dust baths, and they will even bathe in ants, a performance often given by starlings or blackbirds on your very own garden terrace. But all these forms of bathing relate firmly to the process of feather maintenance, they are simply strange manifestations of the pressing need to maintain plumage at peak efficiency.

While it may be pushing it a bit to encourage ants in order to gratify your blackbirds' urge to bathe in them, it is well worth providing a dust bath, which will be eagerly used by wrens as well as sparrows, and gamebirds, too if you are in a suitable location. Dig a pit just a few inches deep and a couple of square feet in extent, then fill it with a mix of well-sifted sand, earth and ash. Have the dust bath in a well sheltered but open place, with cover nearby. The same criteria of shelter and cover apply to your placing of the bird bath. When birds are bathing they may get excited and drop their guard just long enough for a cat to pounce, so make sure there's 10 ft (3 m) or so of open country to give them warning of approaching trouble.

Bird baths and their maintenance

Ornamental, free-standing bird baths on pedestals are poor value from the birds' point of view, though they may well improve the look of a garden – a belief which is well understood by the owners of garden centres! The sides are often too steep and the water too deep. Three inches (7.5 cm) should be the maximum depth, and the access should be by way of a gradual non-slip slope. Birds like to wade in cautiously and do not belong to the ostentatious-plunge brigade. If you are committed to a bird bath which has a slippery, or glazed, surface, introduce some sand or gravel to make life easier for the intended users.

A dustbin lid makes an excellent bird bath, but it needs constant attention. Ponds serve the purpose better.

A long plastic plant tray makes an acceptable bird bath, the sort of thing which tends to be some 3 ft 6 in (1.1 m) long by 8 in (20 cm) wide and up to 2 in (5 cm) deep. Or an inverted dustbin lid will serve perfectly well. Either will be eagerly used for drinking and for bathing by grey wagtails, spotted flycatchers, bullfinches, chaffinches – as well as the usual blue tits, blackbirds, sparrows and so on. But the best material is undoubtedly stone, for instance granite, or concrete.

If the bird bath contains no oxygenating vegetation it must be cleaned frequently, or there will be a build-up of algae which will stink. The water should be changed frequently (daily in hot weather), and must be kept topped up. It is best set up in shade, in the open but within reach of cover and safety.

In cold weather, the ice-free water you put out will be gratefully used. If the bath is of a breakable material, put a block of softwood in it, so that if the water freezes the wood takes the strain. Do not use glycerine or any anti-freeze, which will damage a bird's plumage. It may make sense to cut a piece of thick polythene sheet to line the bath, so that when it freezes you can flip out the ice easily, in order to refill.

Ponds

On the whole, ornamental bird baths are not for the birds. The facilities offered by a natural or semi-natural pond are better by far. Indeed, a pond is almost an essential for any self-respecting bird garden. Properly stocked with oxygenating plants and supporting a healthy population of aquatic insects, snails and crustaceans it will provide clean water for drinking and bathing as well a useful food supply. As anyone with a pond will tell you, it is also an endless source of delight for the naturalist.

There is a good reason for increasing the number of garden ponds, since they to some extent replace the gradual decline in the British pond scene. Once ponds were abundant, serving useful purposes for man as well as supporting a large number of aquatic plants and animals. Village ponds provided water for cattle and ducks, and the passing cart in need of a quick wash. The continual coming and going of the animals kept a weed-free area of open water which is important from the wild animals' point of view, improving the pond's life by diversifying its habitats. Quite apart from the traditional village pond, there were mill-ponds, dew-ponds (set up to serve the distant needs of sheep, and filled by rain, rather than dew) and, indeed, city ponds which served the needs of horse traffic. As time has passed

155

requirements have changed, and most ponds have now been filled to improve the roads. But much wildlife potential has been lost, not to mention character.

Some city ponds remain to give pleasure out of all proportion to the acreage they take up. The pond in St James's Park, London, for instance, is a reminder of the original marsh which was enclosed by Henry VIII to form the oldest Royal Park. The present design dates from the time of George IV, and it has supported ornamental birds since James I. We are told that Charles II used to make a point of going there to feed the ducks.

A pond with healthy vegetation serves birds for both bathing and drinking. Provide a deep end and a shallow end.

Constructing your own garden pond

Garden ponds may not have the noble provenance of St James's, but they will give a full measure of pleasure to the owner. It has to be said, however, that there is a certain amount of hard labour involved in the making of them. A couple of years ago, in connection with the BBC Television children's programme *Wildtrack*, John Downer and I devised a simple pond which could be set up in even the smallest garden. First of all you must choose the site very carefully: it needs to be level, and must be well away from trees so that it gets plenty of sunlight and does not become clogged with leaves in the autumn.

156

The materials required are as follows:

A pond liner, 8 ft 3 in × 6 ft 6 in (2.5 m × 2 m)
Ten wooden stakes
Mallet
Piece of timber, 6 ft 6 in × 2 ft 6 in × 2 in (2 m × 75 cm × 50 mm)
Spirit-level
Spade
Some sand or old newspaper

The pond liner may be bought from a water garden or plastics supplier, but avoid anything less than 1000 gauge $^{15}/_{1000}$ in (0.375 microns) thick as it is easily punctured. There are several kinds:

Black polythene – cheapest type, but has a limited life of about five years unless protected from sunlight by a covering of earth and stones. Use only water-resistant type.

PVC sheeting – more expensive but more resistant to sunlight, best type is strengthened with nylon.

Polyolefin – a high grade plastic liner with a life of over fifteen years.

Butyl rubber – a very flexible rubber liner with a life of over fifteen years. The best quality liner but the most expensive.

If you choose to line your pond with concrete it should be at least 6 in (15 cm) thick and must be sealed with bituminous paint or water-seal cement. But be warned that a concrete pond involves back-breaking work. Our advice is to plump for a Butyl liner, even though it is expensive.

Method

1   Mark out the edges of the pond with stakes; if the ground is not quite level, put the shallow end at the bottom of the slope. Hammer in a stake at each end of the pond using the measurements on the diagram (see page 159). (It's important to keep to these or the liner will not fit.) Rest the wooden beam across the two stakes and mark a point of the beam 2 ft (60 cm) in from each stake. You can find the position of the other stakes by measuring out from these points.

2   You can now start to dig the pond. Put any turves to one side as you can use them later to fringe the pond. Save the topsoil as well, because this will be put back in the finished pond. The best of the soil could be used to make a bank. Put soil to one side, out of the way of the spread lining.

3   As soon as the hole begins to grow, check that the sides of the pond are at the same level by laying the wooden beam over the pond and checking with the spirit level. Take out the stakes and remove the earth from the higher sides.

4   Use the diagram to work out the different depths of the pond. The deepest part of the pond is a third of the way from the end, and the sides of the pond should shelve up gradually from this point to the edge. Do not make the slope too steep. Check the depths are right by measuring down from the wooden beam. If you dig too deep don't worry – you can always put some back!

5   A special feature of the pond is the marshy area at the shallow end. Extend it by removing earth to a depth of 2 in (5 cm) for a distance of 8 in (20 cm) away from that end.

6   When the hole is ready, pick out any stones or sticks which may puncture the lining and carefully pour in some damp sand to make a layer $\frac{3}{4}$ in (2 cm) deep over the whole of the pond. This is to give a soft base for the lining to rest on. If you prefer, you can use sheets of spread-out newspaper, but make sure you build up a good layer.

7   Take the liner, and with it, overlap the deep end of the pond by 8 in (20 cm). Anchor it with heavy stones, temporarily.

8   Spread out the liner over the pond, and push it gently down into the hole. Don't try to make it fit too snugly as the weight of the water will do that.

9   Fill the pond almost to the top with water. You can now see whether you've made any mistakes in levelling the pond. Any errors can be put right by removing or adding earth under the liner. Make sure that there are going to be water levels of from $\frac{3}{4}$ in to 4 in (2 cm to 10 cm) at the shallow end.

10   You should wait two or three days to allow the liner to settle, then carefully trim off the surplus plastic round the edge leaving at least 8 in (20 cm) overlap, but do not cut any off the shallow end. Do not trim too soon, the weight of water drags in a lot of slack. And do not trim too close, or you will have difficulties when arranging your pond surround of stones or turf.

11   Secure the edges of the plastic by burying it under earth or large stones. You can also use the turf for this purpose. If you are using a polythene liner, it's very important to ensure the sheet is totally buried, as in time sunlight will destroy it.

The 'Wildtrack' pond

Prepared
site.

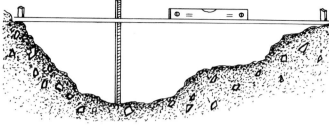

Marking
out.

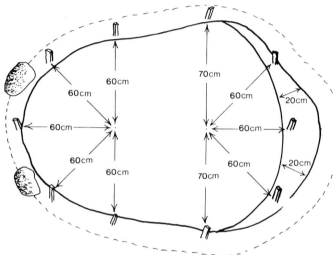

Lining
in place.
Pond filled
with water.

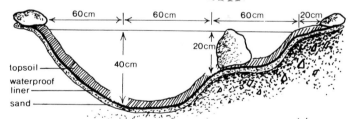

topsoil
waterproof
liner
sand

Planting
the pond.

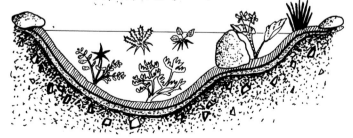

12   Take the topsoil you have saved and sprinkle it over the surface of the pond until you have built up a layer of silt several inches deep over the liner. The earth will form a marshy area at the shallow end. This earth should not be in contact with the surrounding ground or in dry weather water will be drawn out of the pond.

13   Take a couple of large stones, and carefully place them in the shallow end so that they show above the surface. Birds will use these as perching places.

Pond plants

The pond must be properly stocked with suitable plants for it to establish a healthy home for a living community. The plants release oxygen into the water and absorb the carbon dioxide produced by the water animals which are bound to colonise it. They also provide food, shade and shelter for the animals. They thrive on plenty of light, but welcome protection from strong winds. There are three main plant categories, and you should make certain your pond is stocked with some of each.

1   *Free-floating plants* live at the surface, with their roots suspended in the water, eg frogbit, *Hydrocharis morus-ranae*; water soldier, *Stratiotes aloides*; duckweed, *Lemna sp.*; water violet, *Hottonia palustris* – whose flowers are rich with nectar and attract pollinating insects.

2   *Oxygenators* live fully submerged in the deeper part of the pool, some rooted to the mud at the bottom. They are vital, eg starwort, *Callitriche autumnalis*; millwort, *Myriophyllum sp.*; hornwort, *Ceratophyllum demersum*. The starwort is specially valuable because it retains its oxygenating properties throughout the winter. Quillwort, *Isoetes lacustris*, is an excellent food plant from the point of view of fish.

3   *Marginals* live in marshy areas at the edge of the pond and have most of their foliage above water, eg water forget-me-not, *Myosotis sp.*; brooklime, *Veronica beccabunga*; marsh marigold, *Caltha palustris*; flowering rush, *Butomus umbellatus*; slender spike-rush, *Eleocharis acicularis* (this may survive submerged but will then be sterile).

You can find these plants easily enough in wild ponds and ditches, but it is best to buy pest-free stock from a nurseryman (for address see page 181). Follow his instructions in planting. But a general rule is to put the marginals in water 1 in to 4 in (2.5 cm to 10 cm) deep, rooting them in good topsoil.

Common water starwort, *Callitriche autumnalis*, a useful
oxygenator, which will root in the bottom of the pond.

The oxygenators will grow in water 6 in to 24 in (15 cm to 60 cm) deep; if
they need planting (as *Myriophyllum*, for instance), the best method is to
use the specially made baskets which are cheap to buy and allow you to
make subsequent gardening changes easily. A cheaper way is to take a
piece of lead wire and bend it loosely around the base of the plant before
you introduce it to a few inches of topsoil which covers the bottom of your
pond.

Pond animals and visitors

Animals will find their own way to your pond, but it makes sense to
introduce some common water snails straightaway, for they will serve a
useful purpose in grazing the algae. Buy them from your aquarist, and
remember that cheap ones eat just as efficiently as expensive ones.
Ramshorn snails, *Planorbis corneus*, or the freshwater winkle, *Paludina
vivipara*, are the species least likely to attack your 'best' plants. One snail to

161

every 2 sq in of surface water is said to be the desired population, but don't put too many in, they will soon find their own balance.

You may wish to introduce frogs (by way of spawn clouds), toads (spawn strings), water spiders and beetles to suit your own whim. But go easy on the great diving beetle, *Dytiscus marginalis*, if you are going to have largish fish, because it will attack them. And avoid newts in a small pond for they will eat almost anything. Most insect species will find their own way – for instance dragonflies, water boatmen and pond skaters. Sticklebacks and minnows will control the mosquito and gnat larvae which will inevitably appear. Again, a rough rule of thumb is 1 in (2.5 cm) of fish to 24 sq in of surface area. On the whole it is probably best not to have any fish in a very small pond.

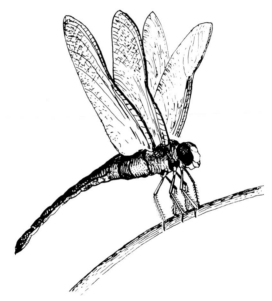

A dozen species of dragonfly may visit the pond for breeding.

Birds will enjoy hunting the pond life, you will enjoy the drama. Robins and blackbirds go for tadpoles, blackbirds try for newts, kingfishers enjoy sticklebacks, and if you are un-British enough to introduce goldfish or carp, then you may be fortunate enough to be visited by a heron. But goldfish are a mixed blessing; they may look colourful but they are bottom feeders, creating in the process a continuous cloud of mud which means the water is rarely completely clear.

Theoretically, the pond should need little maintenance. When it is first filled and planted it will probably be opaque and green-looking for a while, but as the plants grow the water will clear. In hot weather you may well have to add water , especially if you are losing it by capillary action. Devise some way of trickle-feeding it, or diverting rain to it, to save a great deal of trouble. If it is near trees, then fallen leaves may need to be removed in the autumn, but it should not be necessary to clean the pond out. With well-balanced populations a pond will stay healthy for years.

Larger ponds

A pond which can be comfortably jumped across can provide a great deal of enjoyment as well as serving a useful purpose for the birds. But there's no doubt that the possibilities deriving from a larger water area become a great deal more interesting. If you live within reasonable proximity of a wildfowl flightline, by a river valley or water course for example, there is every chance that you will attract breeding or wintering ducks. Even a pool as small as 30 sq ft has attracted flighting ducks, but the larger the better. And if your

A successful pond may attract teal.

163

own home patch offers no chances, then why not cast an influential eye on land owned by public corporations or commercial interests? Over the last few years the great potential of gravel pits in south-east England has been realised, very much to the benefit of water birds and migratory wildfowl.

For a large pond or lake one of the requirements is a deep water area – a depth of over 3 ft (90 cm) – uncluttered by plant growth. This provides for an unimpeded landing place, and also a gathering place for ducklings in the breeding season. Then there must be a shallow area of less than 1 ft (30 cm) depth which allows for plant growth and duckling cover. An island is most important, since it serves as a relatively safe place for resting and preening, and for nest sites. Obviously there must be a reliable source of clean water available from a stream or spring, or the natural run-off from a few acres of grassland, which is itself important for its feeding potential.

If you are starting from scratch, digging is a better construction method than damming, which is an expensive proposition; and, of course, it is better if you are working in flat, open country. If you must dam then it is prudent to check with your local water authority on the legality of your project, and you should get advice from a professional civil engineer. But it seems that the use of a dragline presents the most practical method of pond making, with the built-in advantage that it makes the provision of a central island very convenient, since the machine simply works its way round a perimeter, clawing out great chunks of soil and leaving the central area untouched. Pond construction is dealt with in some detail in a booklet published by the Game Conservancy (for address see page 181).

If your pond has no island, consider establishing a raft which serves much the same purpose in providing a degree of safety from terrestrial predators like rats and foxes. Rafts offer the big advantage that they are immune to changes in water level, and their surface area can be adjusted to suit the size of the pond. They may be constructed of railway sleepers or telegraph poles or even of metal girders on old oil drums. One design involves two 30 ft (9 m) telegraph poles securely moored and held 1 ft (30 cm) apart by struts. A 30 ft × 18 in (9 m × 45 cm) length of Netlon plastic netting is attached underneath, to support a mat of growing vegetation. This practical device will support nestboxes and also acts as a staging post where birds may loaf about or preen. Organise a ramp which will allow easy access for ducklings. Whatever shape or size of raft you devise, it must be topped with soil, giving a home for vegetation such as *Phragmites* reeds and *Juncus* rushes. In turn, these may attract reed buntings and sedge warblers to breed. A successful raft will be well used, not only as a breeding place but as a winter roosting area, especially in bad weather. Rafts may be used by divers, grebes, swans, ducks such as mallards, tufted ducks and goldeneyes, geese such as greylag and Canada, terns, moorhens and coots, offering them safety from predators, shelter from the elements – and a potential house site.

In the case of big ponds and lakes, the associated bankside vegetation can clearly be on a larger scale. When you are dealing with migratory duck, there is a pressing need for seclusion, coupled with shelter from the elements, in the perimeter cover. Waterside cover is well provided by quick-growing birches, and by alder, poplar and the many forms of willow. Some of the most useful willows are:

Creeping willow, *Salix repens.* Low growing, up to 6 ft (1.8 m), usually 1 ft (30 cm), good ground cover.

Common osier, *S. viminalis.* Low screen, up to 18 ft (5.5 m), but can be coppiced and kept at 9 ft to 12 ft (2.7 m to 3.6 m)

Goat willow, *S. caprea.* Female known as pussy willow, with silver catkins. Male has yellow catkins. Plant well back from water's edge, seeds and colonises freely, needs control. Achieves 23 ft to 26 ft (6.9 m to 7.8 m) in height.

White willow. *S. alba.* Common in water meadows. Achieves 59 ft to 66 ft (17.7 m to 19.8 m) in height. Can be pollarded.

Crack willow. *S. fragilis.* As white.

Willows take violent pruning, even to ground level, producing dense scrub. They are easily propagated, as anyone who has hammered in a willow fence post will know.

An outer belt of sheltering conifers provides a desirable shelter belt, but avoid tall trees close to the pond margin, where they will deny much-needed light to the pond plants, and will also over-enrich the pond with fallen leaves. They also represent obstacles and hazards on the final approach to landing for incoming flights of ducks or swans.

Around the edge of the pond itself, you may want to introduce wild celery, *Apium graveolens,* and millet, *Setaria italica,* as well as the *Phragmites* reed beds and sedges which will act as a screen. For these plantings you will be able to collect your material from local ditches and marshes where they are freely available. Take good balls of root, with emergent shoots, cutting back all the aerial growth to encourage shoots and reduce windage during the period of establishment. Plant early in the growing season, from April to mid July, but the earlier the better. In the deep-water areas, introduce pondweed, *Potomogeton natans,* and amphibious bistort,

Polygonum amphibium. This latter plant is invaluable because apart from supporting much underwater life in the summer when it is at the surface, it sinks to reveal a clear surface in autumn, when the ducks need an alighting area.

Fence stock well away from the pond, for they will trample the marginal cover. And make provision for foraging areas and nesting areas, the one needing open grassland, the other secret and sheltered brambly places. Both ducks and ducklings need easy access to both water and land, by way of a gentle sedge slope.

If you hope to attract wild duck, you should bait the pond with corn. Barley is their favourite, and they will enjoy maize once they become accustomed to it. But any grain mix will do, as well as split peas and beans and even more surprising things like raisins and bananas. Potatoes, especially when frosted and mushy, pulped or mashed, are much enjoyed. Scatter this food, mainly over the shallow edges of the pond, as widely as possible. A two-gallon bucket, which holds a dozen pounds of barley, will feed seventy or eighty ducks, especially if the bottom is gravelly, allowing maximum efficiency in food finding. Feed late in the day, a half-an-hour or so before you expect the birds to arrive. The food should all be eaten by the morning. Do not overfeed. Shooting men, who have pioneered the development of duck ponds, tend only to feed during the shooting season, but there's a lot of sense in starting even as early as June, then continuing till the end of winter, even into April, for the best results.

Pochards, and other ducks too, will enjoy your corn.
Barley is the favourite.

SIX
Working for birds

Career opportunities

Birds are a part of our everyday life whether we like it or not – the sparrows which nest in the roof, pigeons which strut the city streets, gulls which defile the newly washed car, or even some unfortunate bundle of feathers brought in and left by the cat. They are the most easily seen and heard of all our wild neighbours and we are involved in their lives through everything we do, interacting with them and all the other creatures of the community. But many people who are keenly interested in birds want a more direct involvement than this passing acquaintance; they are looking for a lifelong career, some part-time work, or a demanding hobby.

A career with birds can encompass an astonishing range of professions and activities, some academic, some manual, some more obvious than others. A good degree in zoology can lead to research into any conceivable aspect of bird life – behaviour, breeding, migration, food requirements or the effects of the weather for example. These things matter to us, as people, because birds are part of our economy. They eat and transport seeds, aid or damage crops, control undesirable insects, cause aircraft accidents by 'bird-strike', provide food for the table for example, thus making jobs available for scientists in the fields of forestry, medicine, agriculture, fisheries, game-conservation, and so on. The top-flight scientists need assistants, laboratory workers and other helpers, skilled and unskilled, academic or manual. A most useful guide and starting point for the kind of job opportunities there are available and the qualifications required for them is the booklet *Careers in Biology*, published by the Institute of Biology (see address on page 181).

Biological work is sometimes pure research – pushing back the frontiers of our knowledge about a bird's life – and sometimes it is motivated primarily by economic requirements, as with pest control or more effective agriculture. Either way, one cannot study birds in isolation – they need to be seen in the context of their habitat. Habitat control and management is probably one of the most exciting and rewarding aspects of nature conservation, affecting the lives and fortunes of all creatures and plants of the community. This is the work of estates and reserve management, and town and country planning for example, and involves people from many fields: geologists and water engineers, hedgers and ditchers, biologists and farmers, foresters, cartographers, and so on. Taken to extremes, at the RSPB's famous reserve at Minsmere, in East Anglia, the low-lying coastal land is managed solely for the benefit of birds. There the skills of those who design and operate the sluices, shift the very soil to make the 'scrapes' and islands, and plan the planting and maintenance of the vegetation are all brought into play. This is exciting work, and although some people argue that it is unhealthy to create reserves specifically set aside from normal everyday activities, such reserves and sanctuaries are probably vital in an increasingly agricultural and industrial country like ours.

Management of this kind is carried out by the RSPB, The Nature Conservancy Council, The National Trust, The Game Conservancy and local Naturalists' Trusts, for example. Such work influences the comings and goings of wild birds, unrestricted in their movements. But there are jobs to do with captive birds, sick and injured birds, and even dead ones. Taxidermy, for example, the work of stuffing the dead skin of an animal, requires an intimate knowledge of the way of life of the subject – how a bird stands, moves or flies – if the final product is to faithfully portray the living version. So, although the taxidermist may deal with corpses, he must study their living relatives in the field.

Captive birds, usually exotic, form a well-known part of zoos and bird collections throughout the country. The inmates must be fed and cleaned, and in some cases serious research and breeding programmes are under way, in an attempt to reinforce natural populations in the wild. Sometimes wild birds become captive for a while, as a result of sickness or injury, and people become involved in their lives in an amateur, as well as a professional, capacity. Birds may be brought in by cats or knocked by passing cars, and although shocked and exhausted they are often uninjured and require nothing more than a period of peace and quiet in a warm, dark cardboard box to restore them to normal. But broken wings, broken legs or damage from oil pollution for example, all common misfortunes, need active treatment. Such birds should be taken to a vet or the RSPCA, or to a reputable bird hospital – many of which are run by private people who devote their time to treating such casualties. Your nearest RSPB branch may be able to help with addresses of such organisations. It is a difficult and time consuming business treating, feeding, housing and rehabilitating birds which have been damaged, or have left the nest prematurely, or been orphaned. And people who undertake such work need total dedication and considerable financial resources. Not a job to be undertaken lightly, or without proper professional guidance.

If you find, for whatever reason, that you have a wild bird in your possession, it is important to remember that in principle all wild birds (along with their eggs and nests) are protected by the law. If, for example, you have cared for an injured bird you are obliged to release it as soon as it is fit enough to fend for itself. There are exceptions to the law, such as those birds classed as agricultural pests (eg rooks and crows) which a farmer is at liberty to shoot; and certain gamebirds can be taken legally at the proper times of the year. Sadly, some people are determined to break the laws of protection for financial gain – selling eggs, taking birds of prey from the nest for the captive market, for instance. If you suspect that the law is being broken inform the police and the Investigations Department of the RSPB. There are proper penalties. The law is quite complicated, involving different schedules, close seasons and so on, but it is fully explained in the RSPB pamphlet, *Wild Birds and the Law*.

To work in direct contact with birds – as a reserve warden, at a bird observatory or at a wildfowl collection – has a tremendous attraction which can be judged by the enormous numbers of applicants for the relatively few jobs available. There are many more opportunities connected with teaching and communicating an interest in, and enthusiasm for, birds, which are just as important as a concern for their welfare. Apart from formal teaching in school – at all levels – we learn about birds through radio and television, books and magazine articles, and museum exhibitions. Such productions all need their teams of workers, from cameramen and photographers to writers and scenemakers, plus artists, taxidermists and so on. All must study their birds, if they are to be successful.

By communicating an enthusiasm for birds and imparting an understanding of their value and importance to the planet, the teachers are laying up treasure for the birds in the future. The RSPB, first formed in 1889 and now with a strength of nearly half a million members and managing 87 reserves, must take a place of honour among the many organisations which work on behalf of wildlife. The RSPB has research scientists, film makers, wardens, and other specialists – full-time staff earning their living with birds – but their great achievement has been to put their subject across to the general public with great enthusiasm through publications, films and meetings.

Leisure time involvement

For most people birds are a leisure time interest – watching them, feeding them and providing sympathetic gardens for them. So for you, with a career quite outside the world of birds, whether retired, working at home, or still too young to earn a living, what are the opportunities for working voluntarily with birds? After joining the RSPB, probably the best way to get involved in your local area is to join the local Naturalists' Trust and Bird Society. There you'll find out what is going on in the area and meet people who will know all about the national bird organisations. Through them your leisure time hobby can be harnessed for valuable and exciting research.

The British Trust for Ornithology is the major organisation which initiates and co-ordinates the sort of research which involves the efforts of a network of birdwatchers covering the whole of Britain. If you want to become actively concerned with census or ringing work, then you need to become a member. The standards are high, the BTO operates to serious scientific criteria, but the range of work is wide enough to encompass everyone from the conscientious beginner to the dedicated professional. The work tends to consist of some form of census – statistical recording of numbers breeding, passing by and wintering – or ringing. And there is no doubt that this work is invaluable. For birds, and bird numbers, are among the most sensitive indicators of the health of our environment. Monitoring fluctuations in their numbers provides essential information to those whose job it is to formulate policy in wildlife conservation. And at the same time keeping a record of your bird observations will give you immense interest and satisfaction.

The garden bird feeding survey

This survey has been running since 1970, organised for the BTO by Pip and Eve Willson. Hundreds of members have been monitoring the effects of providing artificial food at garden feeding stations. The object has been to find out which species visit garden bird tables and when, and what foods they take. In the hard winter of 1978–9, for instance, eighty-three species were recorded at one or other of the 174 countrywide stations. Blue tits, robins and blackbirds were the top three, being recorded at ninety-nine per cent of those feeding places. The range of birds visiting gardens is impressive, including grey herons, grey- and red-legged partridge, water rail,

The British Trust for Ornithology's census of heronries has been carried out annually since 1928. It has been found that there is a higher density of heronries in Ireland than in Britain, although the number of pairs in the colony is lower. The overall figures suggest that England has a higher population, 4–5 pairs per 10 km square to Ireland's 3 pairs. It is thought that the total number of breeding herons in the British Isles is between 7–10,000 pairs.

hawfinch, wheatear and crossbill. It is certainly worth while to keep a record of the birds which visit your own garden. The garden list will vary from year to year, reflecting the weather conditions.

Nest record scheme

The BTO has designed Nest Record Cards which make it possible to record the success, or failure, of known birds' nests. Submitting completed cards to central office adds to the existing body of statistical information on bird-breeding biology – for instance, the timing of each species' breeding season, the number of eggs laid and young reared, and how breeding success is affected by such factors as climate and human activity. Little detailed information of this kind existed before the BTO began the work of completing cards on a large-scale basis, but by 1980 some 567,000 nest record cards had been completed. The information has resulted in many useful publications involving analyses of these records.

OBSERVER R.A. MORGAN **SPECIES** GREAT TIT **YEAR** 1982 **B.T.O.Ref.**

Office Use Only — D / C / H / F

If this record is entered on ATLAS CARD put ✓ in box

COUNTY HERTS

LOCALITY (place-name) TRING Grid Ref SP953108

ALTITUDE above sea level 134 m ✗

HABITAT PRIVATE GARDEN Delete those inapplicable:- RURAL /SUBURBAN/URBAN

NEST SITE NEST BOX ON BEECH

Height above ground or cliff-base 1.8 m ✗

NO. of EGGS or YOUNG at each visit. Record here stage of building; if bird sitting; if eggs warm; age of young; ring nos. etc.

DATE Day	Month	G.M.T.	EGGS	YNG.	
1	MAY				BUILDING STARTED
7	MAY	1600			NEST LINED
14	MAY	1900	6		BIRD ON
21	MAY	1800	8		BIRD ON
28	MAY	1900	3	5	HATCHING
4	JUN	1700	1	7	QUILLS IN PIN
10	JUN	1500	1	7	FULLY FEATHERED
21	JUN	1000	1	0	FLEDGED YOUNG
					SEEN IN AREA.
					ONE ADDLED EGG.

Further visits, notes on outcome, etc. – ON BACK

In the BTO's nest record scheme the success or failure
of each recorded nest is entered on a card.

The common birds census

This is, effectively, a scheme which measures the population changes in a given area over a period of years. This enables the maintenance of an annual index of fluctuations in population levels, and makes it possible to discern trends towards change of status. Originally the census was started, in 1961, at the request of the Nature Conservancy Council, with the emphasis on agricultural habitats, since it is on farms that the use of toxic chemicals and hedgerow destruction has had marked effects on bird populations. More recently other habitats have been covered as well, in order to produce more representative results. The work is exacting, but important, and more help is required if we are to know more about the factors which influence the numbers of our everyday birds.

Other schemes

Other work includes the long-running census on heronries, which aims to count the heron nests at a sample of heronries in the British Isles; wader and wildfowl counts through the winter months; the scheme to map the distribution of every species wintering in the British Isles – the Atlas of Winter Birds. All these are organised by the British Trust for Ornithology. But most county bird societies (obtain addresses from your local library) have census work of some kind in hand, so it is worth checking with them.

Bird ringing

The seasonal movements of birds have always fascinated Man, and he has long sought to unravel their mystery. In part, there is an element of sport in the pursuit, an enjoyment of the challenges offered in trapping and marking the birds, but there is a more serious purpose, that of discovering more about birds' life styles and population dynamics, information which can be of great value in assessing the ecological effects of changes in land use, for instance.

It was in medieval times, somewhere around the twelfth century, that the Prior of a Cistercian monastery in Germany reported that a man who had fixed a parchment to a swallow's leg asking, 'O swallow, where do you live in winter', received a reply in the following spring, 'In Asia, in home of Petrus'. The Romans had long used swallows to carry messeges to their homes, in the style of pigeon post, but it was in 1740 that Johann Leonard Frisch, a Berliner, attached coloured wool to swallows' legs to discover whether individuals returned to the same nest site year after year.

Swallows congregate in flocks before their
long migration journey to South Africa.

In the early nineteenth century, J. F. Dovaston, one of the pioneers of field ornithology, repeated this experiment, fastening cello wire round the swallows' necks. He also attached a copper tag inscribed, in Latin, 'where hast thou gone to from Shropshire?', though sadly he had no returns. Later still, Lord William Percy marked young woodcock at Alnwick, in Northumberland, with more success, achieving fifty-eight recoveries from 375 ringed birds. But his rings were unnumbered and lacked a return address. The credit for the first use of a bird ring which carried its own unique number, and a return address, goes to a Danish ornithologist, H.C. Mortensen, who ringed 164 starlings in 1899. In Britain, systematic bird ringing began in 1909, sponsored by H. F. Witherby in London, the founder of the magazine *British Birds*, and A. Landsborough Thompson in Aberdeen. From 1937 it has been organised by the British Trust for Ornithology.

Trapping, for the purposes of ringing, is based on the methods used by hunters through the centuries, though one of the most ancient techniques, that of liming, is thankfully illegal nowadays. At one time holly bark was stripped in quantities, in the springtime, pounded and mashed by druggists who then supplied the resulting 'birdlime' to hunters. They spread it liberally on suitable roosting-places, where unfortunate songbirds became stuck to their perch. Cage-trapping, decoying, cannon or rocket netting, recordings of bird song—these are all methods used to bring birds to the hand. The most efficient, at the present time, is the use of mist nets made from fine nylon or terylene thread and dyed black. Erected between tall poles to form an almost invisible barrier, they trap any bird which flies into them. The trapped bird may be marked with a brightly coloured dye, which can be seen from a fair distance. However, this method provides only a limited amount of information and lasts only until the wearer moults to a new flying suit. A bird can carry a colour ring which is useful in a limited sense in connection with a small number of individual birds in a relatively restricted area.

Far and away the most useful method of marking is the use of numbered metal rings which carry a return address. In Britain the BTO's rings are engraved with the legend 'Brit. Museum London SW7'. Other countries sport their own legends, every ring carrying a unique group of letters and numbers. The records are computerised and stored according to an internationally agreed filing standardisation, and the coverage is almost worldwide. Both ringing and the photographing of birds is governed by the law as laid down in the Protection of Birds Act, and the primary consideration has always been the well-being of the birds themselves.

To become an accredited bird ringer involves training in stages. With a trainee (T) permit, the holder may only ring birds under the direct supervision of a fully qualified ringer. With a C permit the holder works solo at the supervisor's discretion. After ringing a couple of thousand birds the ringer may achieve either a B permit, which allows him to ring without supervision as one of a ringing group, or an A permit which allows ringing solo in his own name. Endorsements allow the ringing of nestlings and the use of mist nets, which require a high degree of manual dexterity in operation. The BTO publish a rule book – the ringers' manual – but this is not freely available and, it has to be said, the organisation is not looking for new recruits.

The rings come in different metals, from aluminium to monel, and in fifteen different sizes, suitable for anything from a wren to a mute swan. They need to be rugged and abrasion proof, since they may be required to do their job for over thirty years. Seabird rings, especially, must be resistant to corrosion from the elements. The ring is fitted to the bird with the help of special pliers, it rotates freely on the leg, and its weight is negligible by comparison with that of the bird, perhaps 0.2 per cent. Of course, the bird itself would doubtless prefer not to carry it; it is possibly uncomfortable and certainly unsightly. Some birds do accidentally perish as a result of ringing, but the end result, the accumulation of data which would otherwise be unattainable, has to offset the disadvantages. And since ringers are primarily interested in the movements and longevity of normal, healthy birds it is clearly in their interest to devise a ringing programme which has the least disruptive effect.

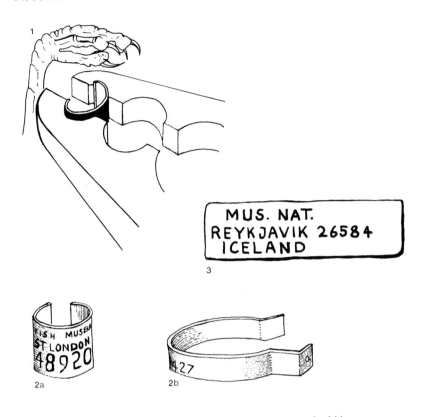

1 A special pair of pliers are required to fit rings on to birds' legs.

2 There are two commonly used types of British ring:
(a) butt rings are used on most British birds
though some of the larger species need to be fitted with a clip variety (b).

3 Most countries have their own national bird ringing scheme.
Depicted is an Icelandic ring flattened out to show full address and number.

In the field, the physical act of ringing is only the first move in a sequence of events which record information. Apart from the ring number, the ringer examines the bird carefully and records its age and sex. (Sexing birds is not always easy, because they carry no external sex organs.) Subtle plumage differences are recorded to do this, and the ringers measure the bird's wing length and weigh it. The ringers themselves find half the cost of running the scheme, the balance is met by the Natural Environment Research Council. At the BTO's headquarters in Tring, the computer now contains over

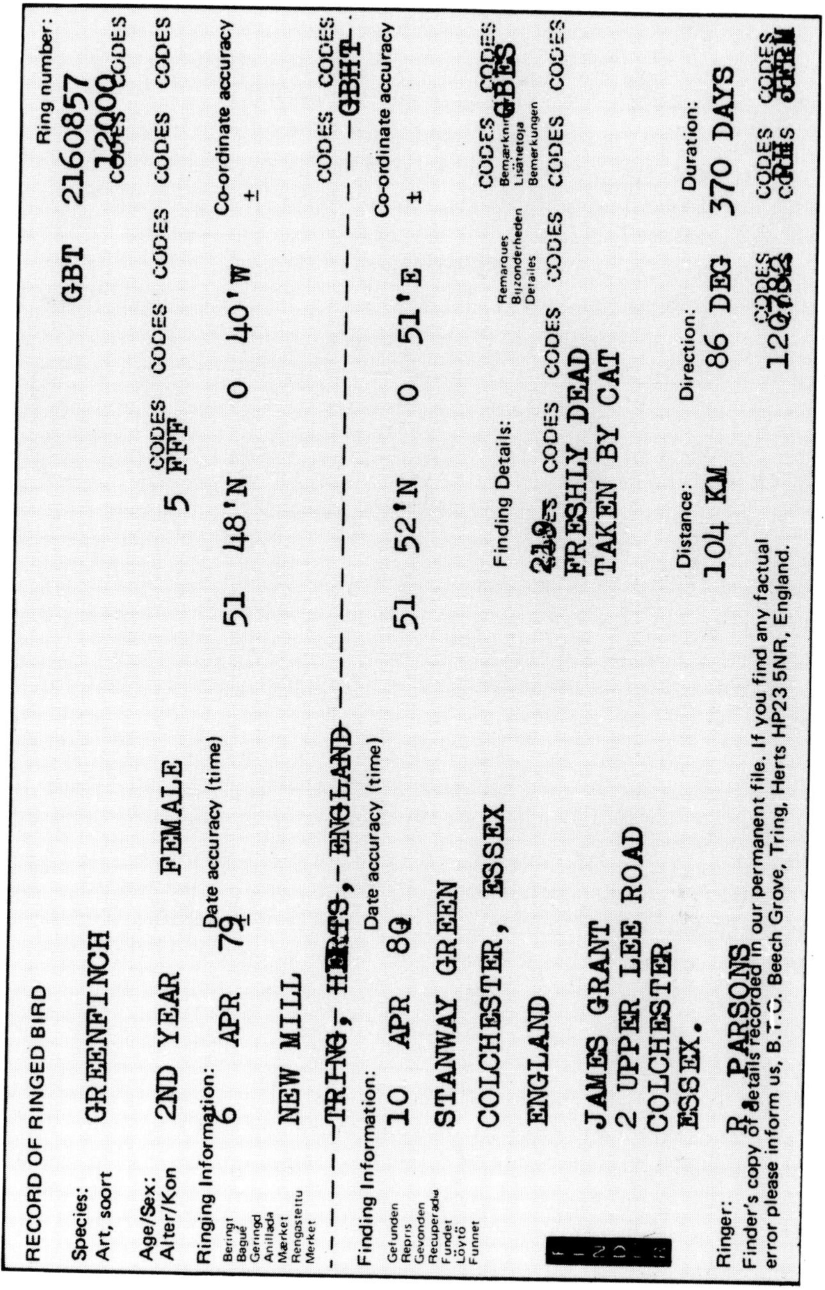
RECORD OF RINGED BIRD

Ring number: GBT 2160857 12000

Species: Art, soort — GREENFINCH

Age/Sex: Alter/Kon — 2ND YEAR FEMALE 5 FFF

Ringing Information: Beringt, Bagué, Geringd, Anillada, Mærket, Rengastettu, Merket

6 APR 79 — Date accuracy (time) — 51 48'N 0 40'W — Co-ordinate accuracy ±

NEW MILL

TRING, HERTS, ENGLAND GBHT

Finding Information: Gefunden, Repris, Gevonden, Recuperada, Fundet, Löytö, Funnet

10 APR 80 — Date accuracy (time) — 51 52'N 0 51'E — Co-ordinate accuracy ±

STANWAY GREEN

COLCHESTER, ESSEX GBES

ENGLAND

Finding Details: 219 FRESHLY DEAD TAKEN BY CAT

Remarques, Bijzonderheden, Details, Bemærkninger, Lisätietoja, Bemerkungen

FINDER

JAMES GRANT
2 UPPER LEE ROAD
COLCHESTER
ESSEX.

Distance: 104 KM — Direction: 86 DEG — Duration: 370 DAYS

Ringer: R. PARSONS 12082 RH

Finder's copy of details recorded in our permanent file. If you find any factual error please inform us, B.T.O. Beech Grove, Tring, Herts HP23 5NR, England.

A bird's history is recorded on this BTO card.

300,000 entries of ringed birds which have been found – the result of many years of dedicated work by the elite band of ringers who have now marked more than eleven million birds in Britain and Ireland.

Once the bird has been ringed and released, the research department of the BTO must sit and wait for subsequent information. Mostly this comes in the form of a letter reporting the bird's death. If, by chance, you come across an avian corpse complete with ring, make a note of the number (send the ring itself, if possible), species of bird (if known) or a description, the place of discovery and the date. Send all this, with any other information you think might be useful, direct to the British Trust for Ornithology (for address see page 181). In due course they will respond with details of the bird's ringing history. Pigeon rings, however, should be sent to the Royal Pigeon Racing Association, The Reddings, Cheltenham, Gloucestershire. If your ringed bird is alive and healthy, simply note the required information and release it!

From ringing records, the BTO has deduced that the roads are a major cause of bird accidents. Twenty-three per cent of barn owls meet their end as a result of collision with vehicles. Otherwise predators such as birds of prey, dogs and foxes account for many, while domestic cats are a major cause of bird death and a helpful source of ring recoveries!

Many and various are the nuggets of information gathered as a result of long-term bird ringing. We know that some birds live long lives, though the average expectancy is very short indeed, especially in the case of songbirds. But an oystercatcher may live thirty-four years, a herring gull, thirty-two. The oldest recorded swallow covered nearly a quarter-of-a-million miles on its migration journeys during its sixteen years of life; an arctic tern, half-a-million in its twenty-seven years. Chris Mead, of the BTO, reckons that the oldest swift, at sixteen, must have flown over four million miles in its lifetime. In cold weather during the winter of 1963, searching for new feeding grounds, a redwing covered 2400 miles in three days. A swift born and bred in Oxford, was recovered in Madrid three days after it left the nest. We know that small birds increase their weight just before migration. A sedge warbler which weighs about $\frac{1}{3}$ oz (10 g) normally, will build up to more than $\frac{2}{3}$ oz (20 g) thus carrying enough fat to fuel a non-stop flight of 2000 miles. They complete this distance in just three days, crossing Europe, the Mediterranean and North Africa, possibly even overflying the Sahara to reach Senegal or Ghana, having slimmed down to half its take-off weight and returned to normal.

Chris Perrins trapped blue tits at a well-stocked bird table and found that it was visited by more than a hundred different individuals in the course of

Sedge warblers may double their weight in a few days before a migration journey which will reduce them to the *status quo ante.*

the morning, while many of us had assumed that our bird table was feeding just the locals.

This mass of information gives muscle to those seeking to influence legislation in a manner which pays due respect to bird requirements, both at home and abroad. Birds themselves recognise no political barriers and need to be conserved on a world wide basis. After all, our ospreys and avocets are shot in Spain and North Africa; and our linnets and redpolls are trapped in Belgium and France while on passage to these shores. And, at long last, we can map the precise routes of the European swallows when they leave us to winter in the south. Our British swallows, for instance, make their way to South Africa, and I have watched them funnelling in to roost in the reed beds of a Johannesburg city park, where the local ringers operate their mist nets.

One of the many pleasures in discovering birds.
A reed warbler perching on *Phragmites* reeds.

Finally, if you enjoy watching the birds, but don't want to become involved in field work, there's plenty of scope for voluntary work in fund raising, selling raffle tickets and cards at Christmas – and all the other ingenious ploys devised to provide the necessary finance for bird reserves and their management. Check with your local Bird Society or Naturalists Trust.

Some useful information

Useful addresses

Royal Society for the Protection of Birds, The Lodge, Sandy, Bedfordshire SG19 2DL. Write for sales catalogue and membership details.

The British Trust for Ornithology, Beech Grove, Tring, Hertfordshire HP23 5NR. Write for list of publications and membership details.

County Naturalists Trusts and Bird Societies addresses are usually available at your local library.

The Game Conservancy, Fordingbridge, Hampshire SP6 1EF.

Institute of Biology, 41 Queen's Gate, London SW7 5HU.

Useful publications

The Birdwatchers Yearbook includes information on addresses and field work possibilities. Published by the Buckingham Press, Rostherne, Hall Close, Maids Moreton, Buckinghamshire MK18 1RH.

British Birds magazine is published monthly. Free sample copy, plus subscription details, from Mrs Erika Sharrock, Fountains, Park Lane, Blunham, Bedford MK44 3NJ.

Suppliers of bird furniture, pond plants, hides, etc

Griffin & George Ltd, Gerrard Biological Centre, The Field Station, Beam Brook, Newdigate, Dorking, Surrey RH5 5EF. Suppliers of pond plants and animals. Send for lists.

John E. Haith Ltd, Park Street, Cleethorpes, South Humberside DN35 7NF. Seeds and foods for cage and wild birds. Send for list.

Nerine Nurseries, Welland, Malvern, Worcestershire WR13 6LN. Bird tables, tit boxes, robin boxes and the useful house martin nests.

Royal Society for the Protection of Birds, The Lodge, Bedfordshire SG19 2DL. The major supplier of bird furniture in the UK. Tried and tested bird tables, nestboxes. Send for catalogue. Highly recommended.

Scandinavian Design, 13 Hillside Road, Marlow, Buckinghamshire SL7 3JU. Glass-sided nestbox, bird tables, feeders, etc. Send for brochure 'garden bird equipment'.

Jamie Wood Ltd, Cross Street, Polegate, Sussex. Suppliers of bird furniture, hides, etc SAE for brochure.

Index